# ENQUIRY

INTO THE

## VALIDITY OF THE BRITISH CLAIM

TO

## A RIGHT OF VISITATION AND SEARCH

OF

### 𝔄𝔪𝔢𝔯𝔦𝔠𝔞𝔫 𝔙𝔢𝔰𝔰𝔢𝔩𝔰

SUSPECTED TO BE ENGAGED IN THE

## AFRICAN SLAVE-TRADE.

---

## BY HENRY WHEATON, LL.D.

MINISTER OF THE UNITED STATES AT THE COURT OF BERLIN—AUTHOR
OF "ELEMENTS OF INTERNATIONAL LAW."

---

## NEGRO UNIVERSITIES PRESS
### NEW YORK

Originally published in 1842
by Lea & Blanchard, Philadelphia

Reprinted 1969 by
Negro Universities Press
A DIVISION OF GREENWOOD PUBLISHING CORP.
NEW YORK

SBN 8371-2072-1

# ENQUIRY,

*&c. &c.*

---

THE message of the President of the United States to Congress at the opening of the present session, states in very brief, but significant and decided terms. the ground taken by the American Government upon the question of the right of visitation and search recently claimed and exercised by Great Britain in the African seas, and other parts of the Atlantic Ocean, which can leave no doubt as to the fixed determination of the cabinet of Washington upon that important subject. It is hoped that the other matters in dispute between the British and American Governments may admit of a pacific and satisfactory adjustment, consistently with the honour and essential interests of both nations.* But the question as to the exercise of the

---

* The author of these sheets has recently published in the "Revue Etrangère et Française de Legislation," &c. an essay upon the incidental question of the criminal prosecution commenced against Alexander M'Leod in the American courts, in which the main question relating to the destruction of the steam vessel, the *Caroline*, by order of the British authorities, in Upper Canada, is also partially examined. This latter point is understood to be included among the objects of Lord Ashburton's mission.

right of visitation and search, in time of peace, upon
the high seas, in respect to the merchant-vessels of
a nation, which has not expressly assented to its
exercise, we fear may be attended with more difficulties, both intrinsic, and those arising from peculiar circumstances in the mutual relations of the
two countries. We say the "question of the *right
of visitation and search*, in time of peace upon the
high seas, in respect to the vessels of a nation which
has not expressly assented to its exercise;" for such,
we shall hereafter endeavour to show, is the true
nature of the pretension set up by Great Britain
on this occasion. It becomes, however, indispensa-
bly necessary, before entering on the question as
to the validity of this pretension, to endeavour to
dispel the thick cloud of prejudice which seems to
rest on the minds of many sincere friends of humanity in Europe as to the principles asserted, and
the conduct observed by the North American nation
and its rulers in respect to the African slave-trade.
Summoned, as it were, at the bar of nations, to
answer the accusation of refusing to sacrifice what
they deem their just maritime rights, for the alleged purpose of suppressing a traffic so justly stig-
matized by every civilized and Christian people as a
crime against humanity,—the people and Government of the United States have a just claim to be
heard before they are finally condemned by the
public opinion of the world on so grave a charge.
Had the allegation of insincerity as to their desire
to contribute by every means in their power, consistently with the independence and honour of their

national flag, towards the final and complete suppression of this odious traffic,—in the guilt of which
both Europe and America too long participated,
though (as we shall also attempt to show) in un-
equal proportions,—had, we say, this allegation been
preferred merely through the British party-press,
the writer of these sheets would not have deemed
it either necessary or proper to take up his pen in
order to vindicate the character of his country from
such a foul stigma. But as the same allegation has
been more than insinuated in public documents, to
which are affixed the signatures of statesmen for
whose character he feels the most unfeigned respect, and in periodical works, understood to represent the views of at least one of the great parties
which divide the British State,—he cannot forbear
from endeavouring to repel what he must regard
as an unjust and groundless imputation. This becomes more especially necessary with respect to
the four great European Powers, who have recently
acceded to the compact proposed by Great Britain
for the alleged purpose of suppressing the slave-
trade, and with whom the United States have ever
been, and still desire to remain, on terms of the
strictest friendship. The maritime resources of
America are not for herself alone: they are for all
who have a common interest in the free navigation
of the seas, and the general balance of maritime
power. When these resources shall be more completely developed, they will, we trust, be devoted,
not to any mere selfish purpose, but to the support
of that great cause common to every civilized and

commercial nation possessed of naval power inferior to the greatest.

As the subject in question has no connexion with the writer's official duties in the particular mission confided to him, he will treat it with that freedom which may become the citizen of a free state, but, at the same time, with all the deference due to those from whom he is constrained to differ, whether official persons or others.

In order to dissipate the prejudices which have gathered over this subject, it becomes necessary to revert to the original progress of the traffic in question, so far as the United States and Great Britain are both concerned.

The testimony of authentic history attests the notorious facts, that the African slave-trade was carried on by the British nation for more than two centuries under the patronage of its Government, and protected by charters of monopoly and public treaties, not for the supply of their own colonies merely, but those of France and Spain, before even the slightest effort had been made to awaken the public mind to a sense of its enormous iniquity. Under the first Stuart kings of England, charters were granted incorporating joint-stock companies, endowed with the exclusive privilege of carrying on trade with Africa. The operations of these companies were sustained by all the power and patronage of the British Government, both in legislative measures and diplomatic acts. The memorable treaty of Utrecht, 1713,— by which the Spanish succession-war was terminated, the balance of power in Europe confirmed, and the maritime law of nations definitively settled,—so far as depending on conventions, granted "to her Britannic Majesty, and to the company of her subjects established for that purpose (the South Sea Company,) as well the subjects of Spain, as all others being excluded, the contract for introducing negroes into several parts of the dominions of his Catholic Majesty in America (commonly called *El facto de el Assiento de negros,*) at the rate of 4800 negroes yearly, for the space of thirty years successively."*

In the debate which took place in the House of Commons on the 16th of June, 1815, relating to the negotiations at the Congress of Vienna respecting this matter, Lord Brougham stated, that "by the treaty of Utrecht, which the execrations of ages have left inadequately censured, Great Britain was content to obtain, as the whole price of Ramillies and Blenheim, an additional share of the accursed slave-trade."

Mr. C. Grant said in the House of Commons on the 9th February, 1818, that "In the beginning of the last century we deemed it a great advantage to obtain by the Assiento contract the right of supplying with slaves the possessions of that very power we were now paying for abolishing the trade. During the negotiations which preceded the peace

* Treaty of Commerce and Navigation, signed at Utrecht, 1713, between Great Britain and Spain, art. 12.—(DUMONT, Tom. viii. P. ii. p. 344.)

of Aix-la-Chapelle we higgled for four years longer
of this exclusive trade; and in the treaty of Madrid
we clung to the last remains of the Assiento contract."*

The principal object, however, of the slave-trade,
so long carried on by Great Britain, was the supply
of her own colonies in North America and the
West Indies. The British settlers in the colonies,
which now form the five southern states of the
American union, were naturally tempted by the
example of the West-Indian planters to substitute
for white servants the labour of African slaves,
better fitted by their physical constitutions to en-
dure the toil of cultivating, under a burning sun,
the rich soil of that region. The desire to obtain
an ample supply of these labourers was powerfully
stimulated by the encouragement of the British
Government, which sought by this means, at once,
to increase the amount of colonial produce for
home consumption and re-exportation, and to discourage the emigration of its European subjects to
the New World, where they were but too much disposed to seek refuge from the oppression of the
Restoration. " On the accession of Charles II.,"
says Davenant, " a representation being made to
him that the British plantations in America were
by degrees advancing to such a condition as necessarily required a greater yearly supply of servants
and labourers than could well be spared from England, without the danger of depopulating his ma-

---

* Walsh's " Appeal from the Judgments of Great Britain respecting the United States," second edition, p. 327.

jesty's native dominions, his majesty did (upon account of supplying these plantations with negroes) publicly invite all his subjects to the subscription of a new joint-stock for recovering and carrying on the trade to Africa."*

The southern colonists yielded with too much facility to the temptation thus held out to them of being relieved from the wasting labour of the field, under a burning sun, and with respect to one particular species of cultivation (that of rice,) in a marshy soil, whose pestilent exhalations are fatal to whites; whilst they were thus left with leisure and the means of providing for their defence against the incursion of a savage foe.† Not so with the settlers of New England. They stood less in need of this class of servants, and therefore, more readily listened to the voice of conscience. The colony of Massachusetts, as early as 1645, enacted a law prohibiting the buying and selling of slaves, "except those taken in lawful war, or reduced to servitude for their crimes by a judicial sentence;" and these were to be allowed "the same privileges as were allowed *by the law of Moses.*" This prohibition, with its exception conceived in the spirit of Puritanism, must have fallen into disuse, since we find that in 1703 the legislature of Massachusetts imposed a heavy duty on negroes imported into that colony. And in 1767 they attempted to

* Davenant's Works, vol. v. "Reflections on the African Slave-Trade."

† Walsh's "Appeal," p. 310.

establish a duty equivalent to the absolute prohibition of the introduction of slaves, which was defeated by the opposition of the council appointed by the crown. Had the bill passed the two branches of the legislature, it must have been ultimately destroyed by the negative of the governor, as all the royal govenors had express instructions from the British Cabinet to reject bills of that description.*

The colonial legislatures of Pennsylvania and New Jersey followed the example of New England in seeking to interdict the farther importation of African slaves by prohibitive duties. But the influence of the African Company, and other slave-traders in the mother country, was ever found adequate to cause their enactments to be rejected by the Crown. It is stated by Lord Brougham, in that celebrated work on the "Colonial Policy of the European Powers," which at an early period of his brilliant career, earned for him the highest reputation in economical science, that "Every measure proposed by the colonial legislatures, which did not meet the entire concurrence of the British cabinet, was sure to be rejected in the last instance by the Crown. In the colonies, the direct power of the Crown, backed by all the resources of the mother country, prevented any measure obnoxious to the Crown from being carried into effect, even by the unanimous efforts of the colonial legislature. If

---

* See Massachusetts Hist. Coll. for Belknap's account of Slavery in that province. See also, Gordon's " Hist. of the Am. Rev." Vol. v. letter 2.

examples were required, we might refer to the history of the abolition of the slave-trade in Virginia. A duty on the importation of negroes had been imposed, amounting to a prohibition. One Assembly, induced by a temporary peculiarity of circumstances, repealed this law by a bill which received the immediate sanction of the Crown. But never afterwards could the royal assent be obtained to a renewal of the duty; although, as we are told by Mr. Jefferson, all manner of expedients were tried for this purpose, by almost every subsequent Assembly that met under the colonial government. The very first Assembly that met under the new constitution finally prohibited the traffic."*

Edmund Burke, in his celebrated speech on conciliation with America, recognised her "refusal to deal any more in the inhuman traffic of the Negro slaves, as one of the causes of her quarrel with Great Britain." And in the first clause of the independent constitution of Virginia, "the inhuman use of the royal negative" in this matter is enumerated among the reasons justifying the separation of the colonies from the mother country.†

* Brougham's "Colonial Policy," b. ii. § i.

† Walsh's "Appeal," p. 317.

In 1772, the Assembly of Virginia presented a petition to the Crown, stating that the importation of slaves into the colony from the coast of Africa had long been considered as a trade of great inhumanity, and under its *present encouragement* they had too much reason to fear would *endanger the very existence* of his Majesty's American dominions; that it greatly retarded their settlement with *more useful inhabitants;* and the Assembly presumed to hope that

It is then not too much to assert that the institution of slavery, which has now become identified with the social system of the Southern American States, was originally established among them by the selfish policy of the mother country, and was perpetuated by the refusal of the metropolitan government to concur in the measures necessary to prevent the increase of the evil by importation. We may even go farther, and affirm, with the able author of the "Appeal from the Judgments of Great Britain respecting the United States," that the institution of slavery would never have existed in the latter, or at least would have been abolished by the

the *interests of a few* would be disregarded when placed in competition with the *security and happiness of such numbers* of his Majesty's dutiful and loyal subjects; and beseeching the Crown to *remove all those restraints* on the governors of that colony, which inhibited their assenting to such laws as might check *so very pernicious a commerce*. Judge Tucker, in his "Notes to the American Edition of Blackstone's Commentaries," from which we borrow this account of the petition, states that he had been lately favoured with the perusal of a letter from Granville Sharp, dated March 25th, 1794, in which he speaks of the petition thus:—" I myself was desired, by a letter from America, to inquire for an answer to this extraordinary Virginia petition. I waited on the Secretary of State and was informed by himself that the petition was received, but that he apprehended *no answer would be given*." —Tucker's *Blackstone*, vol. i. pt. 2 ; App. x. p. 431.

In the Address of the two Houses of Parliament to the Prince Regent in 1819 (hereafter quoted,) on the subject of the slave-trade, it is distinctly avowed that Great Britain " was originally instrumental in leading the Americans into this criminal course." —*Fourteenth Report of the Directors of the African Association*, p. 6.

efforts of the colonies themselves, if it had not been
for the counteracting power of the mother country.
The earliest denunciation of the iniquities of the
slave-trade proceeded from that province founded
by William Penn; and the great English apostle of
abolition has borne testimony to the fact, that the
writings which gave the first impulse to the benevolent efforts of his religious sect in this cause proceeded from the same quarter.*   Long before Clarkson had succeeded in rousing the English nation
from its apathy on this subject,—an apathy which
had been confirmed by selfish class-interests, then
enlisted in *favour*, as they are now enlisted *against*,
the slave-trade, Anthony Benezet, and a crowd of
other American philanthropists, had anticipated his
labours in the same field.†

No sooner was the independence of the Colonies
declared in 1776 than the American Congress passed
a resolution against the purchase of slaves imported
from Africa.   The constitutional powers of this body
did not, at that period of time, extend to a legal prohibition of the importation into the United States,
or of the trade in slaves between Africa and the European West India Colonies.   But the several state
governments of Virginia, Pennsylvania, and New

---

\* See Clarkson's " History of the Abolition."

† Speaking of the combined opposition to the abolition in England, Clarkson says, " The slave-trade appeared, like the fabulous
Hydra, to have a hundred heads ; the merchant, the planter, the
mortgagee, the manufacturer, the politician, the legislator, the ca-
binet-minister, lifted up their voices against its annihilation."

England, passed laws prohibiting both the foreign slave-trade and the importation of slaves under the severest penalties. On the establishment of the present federal constitution, the Congress was invested with the power of prohibiting the foreign slave-trade *immediately*, and the importation of slaves into all the states of the Union *after the 1st of January,* 1808. The abolition of the African slave-trade, so far as American citizens are concerned, was thus made a part of the federal compact, or fundamental law of the Union; and the powers thus given to Congress were exerted in the law of the 22d of March, 1794, which prohibited American citizens from participating in the foreign slave-trade under the penalties of fine and imprisonment from that date, and at the same time anticipated the interdiction of the importation of slaves after the time limited in the new federal constitution. In 1807, laws were enacted by the Congress, on the recommendation of President Jefferson, giving effect to the latter branch of the constitutional power by the actual prohibition of the importation of slaves into the Union after the first of January, 1808. In the same year, 1807, an act was passed which provided that no vessels should clear out on a slaving voyage from any port within the British dominions after the 1st of May, 1807, and that no slave should be landed in the British Colonies after the 1st of March 1808. And yet Lord Castlereagh was heard to boast in the House of Commons on the 9th of February, 1818, that on the subject of punishing the traffic as a crime, Great Britain "had led the way." The truth is, that the American federal government had interdicted the foreign slave-trade thirteen years before Great Britain; that they had made it "punishable as a crime" seven years before; and established the period of non-importation into the Union four years sooner than that assigned by Great Britain for her Colonies.*

Denmark abolished, in 1792, both the foreign slave-trade and the importation into her Colonies,—both prohibitions to take effect in 1804. So that, in fact, America preceded all other nations in abolishing the foreign slave-trade; and all others, except Denmark, in prohibiting the importation, and actually preceded Great Britain in making the traffic a criminal offence.

Nor did the American interdiction remain a dead letter. It has been executed by the penal sanctions provided in the above laws, with the auxiliary aid of a naval force on the American coasts which had been specially provided in the act of 1794. The operations of this force have been since extended to the African and West Indian Seas.

On the 20th April, 1818, an additional act was passed increasing the penalties of the former law. And on the 1st March, 1819, a law of Congress was passed, punishing the offence of importing African slaves with death

The general traffic was afterwards declared to be piracy, by the act of Congress of the 15th May,

---

* Walsh's "Appeal," p. 323.

1820.* But the piracy thus created by municipal statute must not be confounded with piracy under the law of nations. All that is meant is, that the offence is visited with the pains and penalties of piracy.

In point of fact, no considerable *importation* of African slaves into the United States has taken place since it was prohibited in 1808. Public opinion stigmatizing the traffic as a crime against humanity, and the particular interest of the southern states against augmenting the dangerous black population, which already increases by natural means more rapidly than the white, have combined to stimulate the zeal of the public authorities and of the naval commanders to whom this service has been

---

* In the Supplement to the Fifteenth Annual Report of the Directors of the African Association, the committee state:—"America alone has practically seconded our efforts with cordiality. But even this power, anxious as the committee believe her to be in her wishes to destroy this enormous evil, in which too many of her subjects still participate, is restrained by certain constitutional considerations from that full co-operation which is necessary to its effectual repression. If, however, the report shall be confirmed, that she has, by a legislative enactment, stamped the slave-trade with the brand of piracy, and subjected every citizen of the United States, as well as every foreigner sailing under the American flag, who shall be engaged in carrying it on, to capital punishment, she will have elevated her character to a height to which other nations may look with envy; and she will have set an example which Great Britain the committee cannot doubt, will be among the very first to imitate, and which must, sooner or later, become a part of the universal code of the civilized world."—P. 8.

confided. If their efforts have not been completely successful in effectually suppressing the foreign slave-trade, and if some few American vessels and citizens are still employed in transporting slaves from the coast of Africa to Brazil and the Spanish West India colonies, it is owing to the same circumstances which have hitherto baffled the efforts of other governments to prevent such a fraudulent abuse of their flag. The abolition of the slave-trade by Great Britain slowly won its way to public favour through innumerable difficulties, both within and without the walls of parliament. We have already seen what powerful interests, political and commercial, were combined to retard, and if possible to defeat, the measure. The abolition-bill, carried through the Commons by the exertions of Mr. Wilberforce in 1804, was immediately thrown out by the Lords, and the next year was again lost in the Commons. It was ultimately carried under the auspices of the coalition ministry of Mr. Fox and Lord Grenville, who, though transformed into political enemies on the breaking out of the war with France 1793, had ever continued the zealous and eloquent advocates of the abolition. This ministry, which might be considered a happy accident in the progress of the cause, did not long survive the death of Mr. Fox, which followed within a few months that of his great rival. His colleague, Lord Grenville, had barely time to hurry the measure through parliament before the cabinet was dissolved; and it is remarked by Clarkson, that though the bill had now passed both houses,

"There was an awful fear lest it should not receive the royal assent before the Grenville ministry was dissolved."

This fear might well seem reasonable, since, as we are told by Lord Brougham, "The court was decidedly against abolition. George III. always regarded the question with abhorrence, as savouring of innovation,—and innovation in a part of his empire connected with his earliest and most rooted prejudices, the colonies! The courtiers took, as is their wont, the colour of their sentiments from him. The peers were of the same opinion."*

The measure was, at last, reluctantly sanctioned by the Crown; and so long as the mighty struggle between Great Britain and her Continental enemies continued, it was sought to be executed, so far as neutral countries were concerned (except Portugal,) by the exercise of the belligerent right of visitation and search. France, Spain, and Holland, were cut off from participating in the slave-trade by the mere operation of the war itself. The enlightened British cabinet of 1806 foresaw that if they should be able to carry the measure of abolition, the restoration of peace must be coupled with the restitution of the colonies, or a greater part of the colonies, conquered by Great Britain from her enemies, France, Spain, and Holland. In the abortive negotiation for peace undertaken by Mr. Fox in

* Brougham, "Statesmen who flourished in the Reign of George III.," p. 154. Paris ed.

1806, an attempt was made to induce France to join with Great Britain in abolishing the slave-trade. In the account given by Mr. Fox's ambassador, Lord Lauderdale, in parliament, of the causes of the failure of this negotiation, the latter stated, that on his urging with the French ministers, M. de Champagny and General Clarke, the joint abolition of the slave-trade, he was answered, " That England, with her colonies well stocked with negroes, and affording a larger produce, might abolish the trade without inconvenience; but that France, with colonies ill stocked, and deficient in produce, could not abolish it without conceding to us the greatest advantages, and sustaining a proportionate loss."*

In the year 1808, Spain and Portugal threw themselves into the arms of Great Britain for protection against the aggressive attack of Napoleon, under circumstances apparently favourable to the adhesion of these countries to the measures deemed necessary to give effect to the abolition. The relations of peace and amity between Great Britain and Spain being restored, the measure could no longer be executed against vessels sailing under the Spanish flag by the ordinary means of the belligerent right of visitation and search; for the novel distinction of a right to ascertain the character of the suspected vessel, by an examination of her papers and equipments, (which we shall hereafter endeavour to show is a distinction without a difference,) had not yet

* Cobbet's " Parliamentary Debates," 1807, vol. viii.

been invented, or even so much as hinted at in the writings of any British civilian, the decisions of any British judge, or in official documents signed by any British statesman. The abolition could not be lawfully executed against vessels sailing under the Portuguese flag by exercising the belligerent right of search, because Portugal had secured to herself by an ancient treaty, then still subsisting, an exemption from the exercise of the right of search for enemy's property as constantly maintained by Great Britain towards other neutral powers. Reasons of temporary policy prevented the British cabinet of 1808–9 from even remonstrating with the Spanish government of the Cortes against its being carried on under their flag. "It would have been *unwise,*" said Mr. Canning in the House of Commons, "to have taken a high tone with them in the day of their distress; a strong remonstrance on this subject would have gone with too much authority, and would have appeared insulting." But with the feeble and dependent power of Portugal that high tone was actually assumed; and an order in council was issued, authorizing British cruisers to bring in for adjudication such Portuguese ships as might be found carrying slaves to places not subject to the crown of Portugal. Still the traffic continued rapidly to increase, under circumstances of increased cruelty, covered as it was by the flags both of Spain and Portugal. On the 19th of February, 1810, two treaties were concluded, one of alliance and the other of commerce, between Great Britain and the Prince Regent of Portugal, at Rio Janeiro, whither his Royal Highness had fled to seek shelter from the storm of French invasion. By the 10th article of the first-named treaty, the Prince Regent stipulated to prohibit his subjects from carrying on the slave-trade in any part of Africa *not* belonging to him, and within which limits other European powers had renounced it. Great Britain, at the same time, consented to tolerate the traffic in the African possessions of Portugal, in return for other concessions secured to her in the commercial treaty. One of the most important of these was the consent of Portugal to suppress the stipulations contained in the ancient treaty concluded between the English Commonwealth, under the Protector Cromwell, and the Portuguese crown, in 1654, by which the principle of *free ships, free goods*, was recognised by England in favour of the Portuguese flag.* For more than a century and a half this stipulation had continued to exempt Portuguese ships from the exercise of the belligerent right of visiting and searching for enemy's property, as asserted by Great Britain; which power thus rid herself of the last remaining treaty, by which she had been bound to respect the principle of *free ships, free goods*, asserted by most of the Continental nations.

The recent armed neutrality of 1800 had, doubtless, convinced her of the dangers to her maritime ascendancy which lurked under a concession origi-

---

* Schoell, "Histoire Abrégée des Trait's de Paix," tom x. pp. 42–45.

nally made to Portugal as the price of exclusive commercial privileges to British subjects. The treaty of Utrecht, 1713, by which the rule of *free ships, free goods,* had been adopted between Great Britain, France, and Holland, and which had been constantly renewed at every successive peace between these maritime powers down to the French Revolution, was swept away from the European code of public law, by that mighty tempest. On the rupture which took place between Great Britain and Russia, in consequence of the British attack on Copenhagen in 1807, the Russian government published, on the 20th of October of that year, a declaration, "proclaiming anew the principles of the armed neutrality, that monument of the Empress Catherine," and engaging "*never to depart from that system.*" In answer to this declaration, the British government on the 18th December, 1807, "proclaimed anew those principles of maritime law, against which was directed the armed neutrality under the auspices of the Empress Catherine;" and also stated that it was "the right, and at the same time the duty, of his Britannic Majesty to maintain those principles, which he was determined to maintain, with the aid of Divine Providence, against every confederacy whatever."*

This great controversy respecting the rights of neutral navigation thus remained undecided; and Great Britain not only provided, by the treaties of 1810 with Portugal, against the danger which

* Martens, "Manuel Diplomatique sur les Droits des Neutres sur Mer," p. 69.

might lurk in the stipulations of her ancient treaty with the same power, but she secured the incidental means of executing her prohibition of the slave-trade without doing direct violence to Portuguese independence.

Notwithstanding Great Britain thus continued to exercise the uncontested right of search against all neutral powers, and to exclude the flag of her enemies from the traffic in slaves, by the mere operation of the war itself, the annual reports of the African Institution in London conclusively show, that the traffic, thus totally interdicted to British subjects and American citizens, by the respective laws of both countries ; to the enemies of Great Britian by the incidental operation of the laws of war ; and partially interdicted to her allies by special conventional arrangements, continued to be carried on with continually augmenting horrors down to the general peace of 1814, not only under the allied and neutral flags of Spain, Portugal, and Sweden, but in British vessels fitted out in the ports of London and Liverpool under the neutral flag and papers, but navigating on account of British slave-traders.*

The prohibition of the slave-trade by the treaty of 1810 between Great Britain and Portugal was of very little importance, as the Portuguese possessions in Africa, south of the equator, exempted from the operation of the treaty, were precisely the markets to which the slave-dealers principally re-

---

* Reports of 1810, 1811, 1812, and 1813.

sorted for a supply of the wretched victims of their detestable traffic. Sweden was the next power to co-operate in the cause of abolition. The island of Gaudaloupe, conquered from France, was ceded to the Swedish crown, upon condition that the importation of slaves into that colony and the other possessions of Sweden should be prohibited. By the peace of Kiel, concluded on the 14th of January, 1814, Denmark, which had prohibited the importation into her colonies long before Great Britain had adopted a similar measure, was made to stipulate  the total prohibition of the traffic to her subjects.*

Louis XVIII., who had declared that he owed his restoration to the French throne (under Divine Providence) to the Prince Regent of Great Britain, was soon called upon to testify his gratitude by interdicting the slave-trade to his subjects, who had been excluded from it by the operation of the war. He consented to prohibit the importation into the French colonies by foreigners *immediately*,—but insisted on tolerating it for five years longer, in respect to his own subjects, in order to enable the French planters to compete with the British islands, which were already fully stocked.† The British

---

* Schoell, "Histoire des Traités de Paix," tom. xi. pp. 177, 178.

† Schoell, tom. xi. p. 178. In defending the stipulation in the treaty of Paris, signed the 30th May, 1814 (first additional article,) relating to the French slave-trade, against the attacks of the opposition, Lord Castlereagh stated to the House of Commons, that, "However he and the British nation might be inclined to make sacrifices for the abolition, he could assure the House that such was not the impression in *France,* and that even

government endeavoured to tempt France to concede the immediate abolition by the offer of a sum of money, or the cession of a West India island, but without success.*

By the treaty of peace concluded at Ghent the 24th December, 1814, between the United States and Great Britain, the trade was denounced as irreconcilable with the principles of justice and humanity, and the contracting parties mutually agreed to continue to employ their best efforts to promote its entire abolition.

We have already shown that the United States have fully redeemed this pledge.

The Dutch government, by a decree of the 15th June, 1815, prohibited the slave-trade to its subjects, but this prohibition was not then specifically applied to the former Dutch colonies, since they still remained in the possession of Great Britain by right of conquest. By the convention of the 13th of August, 1815, the Dutch government purchased the restitution of their colonies, excepting the Cape of Good Hope and Dutch Guiana, by the entire prohibition of the slave-trade, including the importation into the restored colonies.†

---

among the better classes of people there, *the British government did not get full credit for their motives of acting.* The motives were not there thought to arise from benevolence, but from a wish to impose fetters on the French colonies and injure their commerce."

\* "Ninth Report of the directors of the African Institution," pp. 15, 16.

† Schoell, tom. x. p. 536; xi. p. 179.

Lord Wellington, being reappointed British ambassador at Paris in 1815, was instructed to propose to Louis XVIII. (a second time restored to the throne of his ancestors by the efforts of Great Britain and her allies) the prohibition of the importation of all colonial produce raised in the territories of those countries which had not yet abolished the slave-trade. The proposition was rejected by the French Government, and the whole subject referred to the Congress of Vienna.*

During the negotiation of the treaty concluded at Madrid, on the 5th of July, 1814, between Great Britain and Spain, the British minister, Sir Henry Wellesley (now Lord Cowley,) endeavoured to cause an article to be inserted, by which Spain should prohibit to her subjects both the general slave-trade and the importation into the Spanish colonies. But the British negotiator was only able to obtain from the Spanish government the interdiction to its subjects of the foreign slave-trade to other than the Spanish possessions, the Duke of San Carlos remarking, that when the trade was abolished by Great Britain, the proportion of negroes to whites in the British colonies was as twenty to one in number; that, on the contrary, in the

---

* Schoell, tom. xi. p. 181. The first additional article to the treaty of Paris, 30th May, 1814, had already provided that France and Great Britain should "unite their efforts at the Congress, in order to declare by all the powers of Christendom the abolition of the negro slave-trade as repugnant to the principles of natural justice and the enlightened age in which we live."—MARTENS, *Nouveau Recueil*, tom. vi. p. 11.

Spanish colonies, there were not more negroes than whites; that Great Britain had taken twenty years to accomplish the abolition, from the first incipient stage of its being carried in the House of Commons in 1794 : from which the Spanish minister inferred, that it was unreasonable to require of Spain the sudden adoption of a measure which would be fatal to the very existence of her colonies. After the signature of the treaty, Lord Cowley endeavoured to tempt the Spanish government to concede a point so important to Great Britain, by offering to continue the pecuniary subsidies which the deplorable condition of the Spanish finances might seem to render indispensable. It appears from his despatches that this final effort of the able British negotiator proved fruitless.*

Lord Castlereagh was more successful in the negotiations he undertook with Portugal, and which resulted in the signature of two conventions with that power, signed at Vienna on the 21st and 22d of January, 1815. By this arrangement, Great Britain obtained from the Portuguese government, for pecuniary equivalents, the prohibition to its subjects of the slave-trade on the western coast of Africa north of the equator.†

We now come, in the course of our rapid historical deduction, to the memorable epoch of the Congress of Vienna. The circumstances are notorious which diverted the attention of this great Amphic-

---

* Schoell, "Recueil des Pièces Officielles, tom. vii. pp. 140, 143, 171.

† Martens, Recueil des Traités," tom. xiii. p. 93.

'tyonic council of nations from the readjustment of the maritime and colonial balance of power, and from the renewal of those stipulations in favour of the maritime rights of neutrals which had continued to form a part of the public law of Europe from the peace of Utrecht to the French Revolution. During the abortive negotiation for peace with the French republic at Lisle in 1796, the British negotiator, Lord Malmsbury, proposed to renew, in the projected treaty, the stipulation which had been repeated at every successive peace concluded between France and Great Britain since the treaties of Utrecht, 1713, confirming the various articles of those treaties. The British negotiator stated that great confusion would ensue from the non-renewal of this stipulation. The French Directory, however, rejected the proposal, doubtless from an apprehension that such an engagement might prove inconsistent with the new territorial arrangements which the acknowledgment of the French republic, and its brood of sister republics, would necessarily draw after it. Had either party expected, or sincerely desired peace to be the result of this negotiation, they would probably have more deeply considered the matter. Great Britain might have weighed the light value of such a stipulation in restraining the ambition of France, whilst France might have considered the renewed acknowledgment of the principle of *free ships*, *free goods*, by the British government, as of much more importance to the maritime interests of France than the mere possible inferences respecting the Continental balance of

power which might be drawn from the renewal of
the treaties of Utrecht. Be this as it may, it could
not be expected that the monarchs assembled at
Vienna, owing so deep a debt of gratitude to the
British government for its strenuous resistance to
" the enemy of Europe," and disturbed as they were
in the midst of their deliberations by the reappear-
ance of their common foe on the scene of action,
could think of providing against the possible abuse
of the immense maritime resources and naval power
which the results of the war had left in the hands
of Great Britain, and which she had taken care to
secure by separate treaties of peace with the maritime states, her late enemies. Nor could it be expected that the allied sovereigns would deny to
Great Britain almost any concession in favour of
her colonial interests, which did not directly affect
in an injurious manner the commercial interests of
those Continental states who possessed no colonies.
This was more especially to be looked for when
such concessions should be demanded in the name
of humanity and of the sacred cause which had so
long and deeply engaged the affections of philanthropists throughout the Christian world. The only
wonder is, after all, that some more decisive measure was not obtained by Lord Castlereagh from
the Congress than the declaration of the 15th February, 1815, denouncing the African slave-trade
"as inconsistent with the principles of humanity
and universal morality," and, at the same time,
leaving every state at liberty to determine for itself,
or by negotiation with others, the period when the

odious traffic should be finally abolished. Even this qualified denunciation of the traffic encountered serious opposition from the ministers of Spain and Portugal, who absolutely refused to listen to the renewal of the same proposition which had been before made at Paris, that in case the trade should be still continued by any state beyond the term justified by real necessity, the dissent of such state should be punished by the prohibition of the importation, into the dominions of all the powers represented in the Congress, of colonial produce, the growth of any colony where the trade should still continue to be tolerated; and that they should only permit the introduction of the products of such colonies where the trade was unlawful; "or," as the protocol stated, "those of the vast regions of the globe which furnish the same productions by the labour of their own inhabitants."*

The ministers of Spain and Portugal declared that the introduction of such a system would give rise to reprisals on the part of any State to which it might be applied; and they urged in favour of the farther continuance of the traffic in human flesh by their countrymen, that the British colo-

* Schoell, " Histoire des Traités de Paix," tom. x. pp. 187, 188. " These *vast regions*," says Schoell, " refer to the British possessions in the East Indies, the interest of which, though their express mention was studiously avoided in the negotiation, was found to conform to the *principles of humanity and religion*. Europe will one day become tributary to these countries, when the plantations of the West Indies shall be deserted for want of hands to cultivate them."

nies were fully stocked with slaves during the long interval which elapsed from the first authentic proposal until the final adoption of the measure of abolition by Great Britain; whilst the colonies of Cuba and Porto Rico had been cut off, during all that period, by the war, from recruiting their slave population; and the vast regions of Brazil still required an annual supply from the African coast to keep up its cultivation.

The result was that Lord Castlereagh completely failed in his endeavours to obtain the *immediate* abolition, or to shorten the period for which the trade should be carried on by France, Spain, and Portugal. France still insisted on continuing it for five years, nor could the Spanish and Portuguese Governments be prevailed upon to fix a shorter period than eight years.*

What the British Government could not persuade the Bourbons to do, the Emperor Napoleon spontaneously did, on his return from Elba, by his decree, March, 1814, immediately abolishing the slave-trade in France and her colonies.† This decree, wedged in between the first and second restorations, must evidently be considered as a desperate attempt to conciliate England at that critical period of his fortunes; since, in the zenith of his

* Ninth Report of the Directors of the African Institution, pp. 18, 19. Klüber, Acten des Wiener Congresses, bd. iv. s. 531.

† Ninth Report of the Directors of the African Institution, Appendix C. p. 83.

power, he had, as we have already seen, absolutely refused the concession as fatally injurious to the colonial interests of France.* Louis XVIII., on his return from Ghent, could do no less than confirm the Imperial measure, by a formal assurance that "the trade was henceforth for ever forbidden to all the subjects of his most Christian Majesty," under the hand of that same Prince Talleyrand, who once said that "language was given to man to conceal his thoughts." Whether the Bourbon kings of the elder branch had conceived inveterate prejudices against the abolition, as a dream of revolutionary philosophy which had been fearfully realized in the bloody catastrophe of the flourishing colony of St. Domingo, or whether they consulted merely the feelings and supposed commercial interests of their subjects, it would be superfluous to inquire. It is, however, certain that the pretended abolition

* In their Tenth Report, 27th of March, 1816, the Directors of the African Institution state that "the gratification they felt in being able to lay before the subscribers the memorable denunciation of the slave-trade by the Powers assembled in Congress at Vienna, was greatly damped by the consideration that all these measures, however wisely planned or unceasingly urged, had proved ineffectual; and that the French Government had determined to retain their slave-trade for the full term allowed by the treaty of Paris. Very soon, however, after the declaration of the Congress, there arose a cloud in the political horizon, which seemed to threaten desolation to the civilized world. Yet, amidst this gloom, a beam of light unexpectedly shone upon Africa. No sooner had Buonaparte regained for a season the government of France, than he issued a decree for the immediate and total abolition of the French slave-trade."

remained for a long time unexecuted under the government of the Restoration.*

It was during the negotiations undertaken by the British Government with the French cabinet, after the peace of 1814, that we first hear of the proposition to concede the mutual right of search as the only effectual means of suppressing the trade. The Duke of Wellington proposed it to Prince Talleyrand, but soon discovered "that it was too disagreeable to the French Government and nation to admit of a hope of its being urged with success."†

By the treaty of Madrid of the 22d of September,

---

* Eleventh Report of the Directors of the African Institution, pp. 1–10. Memoranda relating to the slave-trade in France in 1820.

† Duke of Wellington's Despatch to Lord Castlereagh, 5th November, 1814.

Mr. Berryer, in his Speech in the Chamber of Deputies, January 24, stated that "the Duke of Wellington communicated on the 26th of August, 1814, to the king's ministry a memoir tending to establish the principle of the abolition of the Negro slave-trade; and, as a means of effecting this object, he demanded, among other things, that there should be granted to the ships of war of both nations, north of the equator, and to the twenty-fifth degree of west longitude from the meridian of Greenwich, the permission to visit the merchant-vessels of both nations, and to carry into port such, on board of which slaves should be found, there to be confiscated according to the laws of the state to which they might belong."

M. de Talleyrand answered, in the name of the King of France, that he would never admit any other maritime police than that which each power exercised on board its own vessels.—*Journal des Débats*, January 25, 1842.

1817, Great Britain purchased from Spain the immediate abolition of the trade north of the equator, and a promise to abolish it entirely after the year 1820, for the sum of 400,000*l.* Mr. Wilberforce stated, during the discussion of the treaty in the House of Commons on the 9th of February, 1818, the great advantages of this bargain : " He could not but think that the grant to Spain would be more than repaid to Great Britain in commercial advantages by the opening of a great continent to British industry,—an object which would be entirely defeated if the slave-trade was to be carried on by the Spanish nation. Our commercial connexion with Africa will much more than repay us for any pecuniary sacrifices of this kind. He himself would live to see Great Britain deriving the greatest advantages from its intercourse with Africa."

The treaty of Madrid also contained the so muchdesired concession of the right of search, which had, in the meantime, been yielded by Portugal, as to the trade interdicted by her north of the equator. During the same debate above referred to, great satisfaction was expressed with this arrangement. "The introduction of the right of search, and of bringing in for condemnation in time of peace, was declared to be a *precedent* of the utmost importance."*

Lord Castlereagh determined to avail himself of this " precedent" without delay. He assembled the ministers of the principal maritime powers of Europe in London in the month of February 1818, and laid before them a paper, stating that since the

* Walsh's " Appeal," p. 376.

peace a considerable revival of the slave-trade had taken place, especially north of the equinoctial line, and that the traffic was principally of the illicit description. That as early as July 1816, a circular intimation had been given to all British cruisers, *that the right of search, being a belligerent right, had ceased with the war.* That it was proved beyond the possibility of doubt, that unless the right to visit vessels engaged in the slave-trade should be established by mutual concessions on the part of the maritime states, the illicit traffic must not only continue to exist, but must increase. That even if the traffic were universally abolished, and a single state were to refuse to submit its flag to the visitation of the vessels of other states, nothing effectual would have been done. That the plenipotentiaries ought, therefore, to enter into an engagement to concede mutually the right of search, *ad hoc*, to their ships of war.

The ministers of the different maritime powers of the European continent assembled in the conference, could not, of course, do more than engage to transmit this proposition to their respective courts.*

On the 21st of February, 1818, Lord Castlereagh addressed Sir Charles Stuart, the British ambassador at Paris, a despatch, accompanied with a memorandum laid before the conference of London, with instructions to endeavour to obtain the assent of the French Government to concur in adopting, with a view to the more effectual suppression of the slave-

* Thirteenth Report of the Directors of the African Institution, pp. 3–11.

trade, the mutual right of search which had been conceded by Spain, Portugal, and the Netherlands. But the proposition was rejected by the Duke of Richelieu, on the ground that "the offer of reciprocity would prove illusory; and that disputes must inevitably arise from the abuse of the right, which would prove more prejudicial to the interests of the two governments than the commerce they desired to suppress."*

The American minister was, of course, not invited to the above conference. The United States have hitherto, wisely as they believe, avoided as far as possible entangling themselves in the complicated international relations of Europe and the inextricable labyrinth of European politics. Instead of appearing in the great Amphictyonic councils of European nations, where they might be outvoted by a preponderance of interests and views having no connexion with their policy, they have, in general, abstained from mixing up their concerns with those of the Old World. This policy, of course, may admit of exceptions, which will probably hereafter be multiplied as the facilities of intercourse between the two continents of Europe and America are increased, and their respective commercial and political interests become more blended together. But the subject now under consideration was not deemed by the American cabinet of 1818, over which then presided that most prudent of statesmen, Mr. Monroe, to constitute an exception to those general rules which

* Supplement to the Fifteenth Annual Report of the Directors of the African Institution, p. 77.

had been laid down by Washington, and ever since undeviatingly pursued by the illustrious men his successors, without distinction of domestic party.

Such being the known disposition of the United States' government, the proposal in question was communicated by Lord Castlereagh to Mr. Rush, the American minister in London, together with the treaties then recently concluded by Great Britain with Spain, and other European powers, conceding the right of search under certain regulations, and inviting the American Government to join in the same, or like arrangements. Mr. Rush took the communication *ad referendum* to his government.

In the reply of Mr. Secretary Adams to Mr. Rush's despatch on this occasion, the latter was directed by the President to give the strongest assurances to the British Government that the solicitude of the United States for the accomplishment of the common object—the total and final abolition of the slave-trade—continued with all the earnestness that had ever distinguished the course of their policy in respect to that odious traffic. As a proof of this continued earnestness, Mr. Rush was desired to communicate to that government a copy of the act of Congress then just passed (act of the 20th of April, 1818,) in addition to the prohibitory law of 1807; and to declare the readiness of the American Government to adopt any farther measures, within their constitutional power, which experience might prove to be necessary for the purpose of attaining so desirable an end.

But on examining the treaties communicated by

Lord Castlereagh, it would be observed that all their essential provisions appeared to be of a character not capable of being adapted to the institutions or the circumstances of the United States.

The power agreed to be reciprocally given to officers of the ships of war of either party to enter, search, capture, and carry into port for adjudication the merchant-vessels of the other, however qualified and restricted, is most essentially connected with the establishment by each treaty, of two mixed courts, one of which to reside in the external or colonial possessions of each of the two parties, respectively. This part of the system was indispensable, to give it that character of reciprocity without which the right granted to the armed ships of one nation to search the merchant-vessels of another would be rather a mark of vassalage than of independence. But to this part of the system the United States, having no colonies, either on the coast of Africa or in the West Indies, could not give effect.

Mr. Rush was instructed to add that, by the American constitution, it was provided that the judicial power of the United States should be vested in a supreme court, and in such inferior courts as the Congress might from time to time, ordain and establish. It provided that the judges of these courts should hold their offices during good behaviour, and that they should be removeable by impeachment and conviction of crime or misdemeanour. There might be some doubt whether the constitutional power of the federal government was competent to institute a court for carrying into execution their penal statutes beyond the territories of the United States,—a court consisting partly of foreign judges not amenable to impeachment for corruption, and deciding upon the statutes of the United States without appeal.

It was farther stated, that the disposal of the negroes found on board the slave-trading vessels, which might be condemned by these mixed courts, could not be carried into effect by the United States; for, if the slaves of a vessel condemned by the mixed court should be delivered over to the United States' government as free men, they could not, but by their own consent, be employed as servants or free labourers. The condition of the blacks in the American Union being regulated by the municipal laws of the separate states, the United States' government could neither guarantee their liberty in the States where they could only be received as slaves, nor control them in the States where they would be recognised as free.

That the admission of a right in the officers of foreign ships of war to enter and search the vessels of the United States, in time of peace, under any circumstances whatever, would meet with the universal repugnance in the public opinion of that country. That there would be no prospect of a ratification, by the advice and consent of the senate, to any stipulation of that nature. That the search by foreign officers, even in time of war, was so obnoxious to the feelings and recollections of the country, that nothing could reconcile them to the extension of it, to a time of peace, however qualified or restricted. And that it would be viewed in a still more aggravated light, if, as in the treaty with the Netherlands, connected with a formal admission that even vessels under convoy of ships of war of their own nation should be liable to search by the ships of war of another.

Mr. Rush was therefore, finally, instructed to express the regret of the ·President, that the stipulations in the treaties communicated by Lord Castlereagh were of a character to which the peculiar situation and institutions of the United States did not permit them to accede. The constitutional objection might be the more readily understood by the British cabinet, if they were reminded that it was an obstacle proceeding from the same principle which prevented Great Britain, formally, from being a party to the Holy Alliance; neither could they be at a loss to perceive the embarrassment under which the American Government would be placed by receiving cargoes of African negroes under the obligation of guaranteeing their liberty and employing them as servants. Whether the British cabinet would be as ready to enter into the feelings of the American Government with regard to the search by foreign navy lieutenants of vessels under convoy of American naval commanders, was, perhaps, of no material importance. The other reasons were presumed to be amply sufficient to convince them that the motives for declining this overture were compatible with an earnest wish that the measures concerted by these treaties may prove successful in extirpating that root of numberless evils, the traffic in human blood ; and that they were also compatible with the determination of the American Government to co-operate, to the utmost extent of its constitutional powers, in this great vindication of the sacred rights of humanity.*

It will thus be perceived that the proposition made by Lord Castlereagh to the American Government to concede the right of search as the only effectual means of attaining the common end both governments equally desired to attain, was courteously, but peremptorily, rejected by the American cabinet. The pretension of exercising that right upon American vessels, in any form, however mitigated, and under any name, however adapted to conceal its real character, without the express consent of the United States, was not then even so much as hinted at by a British statesman, not wanting in bold daring on occasions suitable to the display of that quality. But Lord Castlereagh, with all his political courage, was a man of too much sagacity not to perceive that the deep wounds inflicted by the abuse of the right of search, which had produced the war between the two countries, then so recently terminated, were still too fresh to allow the American Government, even if it had been so disposed, to allow of its revival in any shape and for any purpose, even by compact, much

* Mr. John Quincy Adams' Despatch to Mr. Rush, November 2, 1818. American "State Papers" (foreign relations,) vol. iv. p. 339.

less to submit to its gratuitous assumption in time of peace. When the Spanish treaty was laid before Parliament, his lordship stated that " The illicit traffic arose out of the partial abolition, and out of the facilities created by the cessation of belligerent rights in consequence of the peace. It was for the first time, he believed, in diplomatic history that the states of Europe had bound themselves by a mutual stipulation to exercise the right of search over their respective merchantmen with a view of giving effect to this laudable object. They had now arrived (said he) at the last stage of their difficulties and the last stage of their exertions. One great portion of the world was rescued from the horrors of the traffic. The approval of the grant amounted to this, whether the slave-trade should be entirely abolished or not?"*

Fortified with this concession, thus purchased from Spain, Lord Castlereagh repaired to the Congress of Aix-la-Chapelle, whither he was followed by Mr. Clarkson, the great apostle of abolition. The latter presented in November, 1818, an eloquent memorial to the assembled sovereigns, which was supported by the former with the whole weight of the power and influence of Great Britain. This paper stated that, "In point of fact, little or no progress had been made in practically abolishing the slave-trade. That all the declarations and engagements of the European powers as to abolition, must prove perfectly unavailing, unless new means were

* British Annual Register, vol. lx. p. 19.

adopted." The British minister, therefore, proposed, as the only means left of accomplishing the object avowed by the Congress of Vienna, 1st, The general concession of a reciprocal right of search and detention for trial, applicable to the merchant-vessels of all nations who had prohibited the trade; 2d, The solemn proscription of the trade as piracy under the law of nations.

These proposals were answered by the Plenipotentiaries of the five great European powers in separate notes. France peremptorily rejected both proposals, and suggested, as a counter *projet*, a plan of common police for the *surveillance* of the trade, by which the several powers would be immediately informed of the transactions of each other with respect to it, and of all abuses practised within the limits of their respective jurisdictions.

The proposal to declare the trade piracy under the law of nations was also rejected by the three great powers, Austria, Prussia, and Russia. "It was evident," said the latter, "that the general promulgation of such a law could not take place until Portugal had totally renounced the trade."

The above three powers also concurred with France in rejecting the British proposal as to the right of visitation and search. The answer of the Russian Plenipotentiary, Count Nesselrode, stated that it appeared to the Russian cabinet, beyond all doubt, that there were some states whom no consideration would induce to submit their navigation to a principle of such great importance as the right of visitation and search (*droit de visite.*) He, therefore, proposed, in lieu of the British *projet*, the establishment of " an institution, situated at a central point on the western coast of Africa, in the formation of which all the states of Christendom should take a part. This institution being declared for ever neutral, separated from all political and local interests, like the fraternal and Christian alliance, of which it would be a practical manifestation, would pursue the single object of strictly maintaining the execution of the laws. The institution would consist of a maritime force, composed of an adequate number of ships of war appropriated to the service; of a judicial power, which should adjudicate on all criminal offences relating to the trade, according to a code of legislation on the subject established by the common wisdom; of a supreme council, in which would reside the authority of the institution, which would regulate the operations of the maritime force, would revise the sentences of the federal tribunals, would cause them to be executed, would inspect all details, and would render an account of its administration to future European conferences. The right of visiting and detaining for trial would be granted to this institution, as the means of fulfilling the end of its establishment; and, perhaps, no maritime nation would refuse to submit its flag to the jurisdiction of this police, exercised in a limited and clearly defined manner, and by a power too feeble to be abused, too disinterested on all maritime and commercial questions, and, above all, too widely combined in its elements not to observe a severe but impartial justice towards all."*

It may easily be anticipated by the reader that neither the French nor the Russian substitute for the British *projet* was acceptable to Lord Castlereagh. He proposed a counter *projet* limiting the exercise of the right of search demanded to a term of years. " He flatters himself," says the thirteenth Report of the African Institution, " that he has made a considerable impression in removing the strong repugnance which was at first felt to the measure."†

All that could be obtained from the Congress of Aix-la-Chapelle was a declaration that " the negro slave-trade was an odious crime, the disgrace of civilized nations, and that it was a matter of urgency to put an end for ever to this scourge which had so long desolated Africa, degraded Europe, and afflicted humanity."‡

The next we hear of this attempt to incorporate into the maritime code of nations "a principle of such great importance," as it was termed in the above note of the Russian plenipotentiary at Aixla-Chapelle, was at the Congress of Verona. In the despatch addressed on the 1st of October, 1822, by Mr. Canning (who had become Secretary of State

* Thirteenth Report of the directors of the African Institution, pp. 23–25.

† Report, pp. 1–3

‡ Fourteenth Report of the Directors of the African Institution, p. 1.

for Foreign Affairs in the place of the Marquess of Londonderry,) to the Duke of Wellington, British Ambassador at the Congress, it was stated that whatever might be the advantage or disadvantage to the British colonies, it was much to be feared that, to Africa, the abolition by Great Britain had been an injury rather than a gain. The slave-trade, so far from being diminished in extent by the exact amount of what was in former times the British demand, was, upon the whole, perhaps, greater than at the period when that demand was the highest; and the aggregate of human sufferings, and the waste of human life in the transportation of slaves from the coast of Africa to the colonies, were increased in a ratio enormously greater than the increase of positive numbers. Unhappily, it could not be denied that their very attempts at prevention, imperfect as they yet were, under the treaties which then authorized their interference, tended to the augmentation of the evil. The dread of detection suggested expedients of concealment productive of the most dreadful sufferings to a cargo, with respect to which it hardly ever seems to occur to its remorseless owners that it consists of sentient beings. The numbers put on board in each venture were so far from being proportioned to the proper capacity of the vessel, that the probable profits of each voyage were notoriously calculated only on the survivors; and the mortality was accordingly frightful, to a degree unknown, since the attention of mankind had been first called to the horrors of this traffic.

Mr. Secretary Canning added, that to these enormous and, he feared, even growing evils, they had nothing to oppose but the declaration of the Congress of Vienna; their treaties with Spain and the Netherlands, abolishing the trade definitively and totally, and that with Portugal restricting the Portuguese slave-trade to the south of the line. It was the truth (however lamentable or incredible) that, by the testimony of the French Government itself, there was no public feeling on this subject in France which responded, in the smallest degree, to the sentiment prevalent in England; that no credit was given to the people or the legislature of that country for sincerity in those sentiments; that their anxiety on the matter was attributed to a calculation of national interest; and that a new law, founded on a proposition from England for new restrictions on the illicit slave-trade, would at this moment be thrown out in the legislature of France.

The principal advantage, then, to be derived from the union of sovereigns at Verona, according to Mr. Secretary Canning, appeared to resolve themselves into the following :—

1. An engagement on the part of the Continental sovereigns to mark their abhorrence of this accursed traffic, by refusing admission into their dominions of the produce of colonies belonging to the powers who had not abolished, or who notoriously continued, the slave-trade.

2. A declaration in the names, if possible, of the whole alliance ; but, if France shall decline being a party to it, then in the names of the three other powers (Austria, Prussia, and Russia,) renewing

the denunciation of the Congress of Vienna, and exhorting the maritime powers who had abolished the slave-trade to concert measures among themselves for proclaiming and treating it as piracy, with a view of founding upon the aggregate of such separate engagements between state and state a general engagement to be incorporated into the public law of the civilized world.

Such a declaration, it was added, as it assumed no binding force, would not be obnoxious to the charges which would attach to the introduction of a new public law by an incompetent authority; while, at the same time, its moral influence might materially aid the British cabinet in its negotiations with other maritime states. It could have no difficulty in consenting that subjects of the United Kingdom found trading in slaves should be treated as pirates, upon a reciprocal admission of the same principle by other powers.

All the powers assembled in the Congress united in declaring their continual adherence to the principles in favour of which they had pronounced themselves since the Congress of Vienna; and it was agreed to record anew these principles by a declaration analogous to that of the 8th February, 1815. But the particular practical measures proposed by the British plenipotentiary to give effect to this renewed profession of principles, were taken *ad referendum* by the other plenipotentiaries, except those of France, for the farther deliberations of their respective courts.

The plenipotentiaries of France, MM. de Chateaubriand and de Caraman, explicitly rejected these measures in a detailed answer to the Duke of Wellington's memorandum, in which, after avowing that "the French Government participated in the solicitude of the British Government to suppress a traffic equally reprehensible in the eyes both of God and man," they proceeded to develope the causes which rendered public opinion less decided on this subject in France than in Great Britain. A people so humane, so generous, and so disinterested as that of France—a people always ready to furnish the example of submitting to sacrifices—deserved to have explained what might appear an inexplicable anomaly in their character.

The massacre of the colonists of St. Domingo, and the burning of their habitations, left, in the first instance, painful recollections among those families who lost relations in those sanguinary revolutions. It might be permitted to call to mind these calamities of the *whites*, when the British memorandum painted with so much truth and force of colouring, the sufferings of the *blacks*, in order to prove that every thing which excites pity naturally influences public opinion. It was evident that the abolition of the slave-trade would have been less popular in England, if it had been preceded by the ruin and murder of the British colonists in the West Indies.

It might farther be remarked that the abolition of this traffic was not decreed in France by an act of national legislation discussed in the Tribune.

It was the result of a stipulation in the treaty by which France had atoned for her victories. From that moment the measure was coupled in the eye of the multitude with foreign considerations, merely because they believed it to be imposed upon them; and it, therefore, became subjected to that unpopularity which must ever attend measures of compulsion. The same thing would have happened in any country where public spirit and a proper degree of national pride are found to exist.

A motion in the British Parliament, ever honourable to its philanthropic author, was finally crowned with success; but this triumph was achieved after repeated rejections of the proposed measure, although supported by one of the greatest ministers England ever produced. During these protracted debates, public opinion had time to ripen and to come to an ultimate decision. The commercial interest, which foresaw the result, had time to take its precautions; a number of negroes, exceeding the wants of the colonists, were transported to the British islands; and successive generations of slaves were thus provided to fill up the void to be occasioned by the abolition of the traffic when it should take place.

No such advantage was possessed by France. The first convention on this subject between France and Great Britain after the restoration, recognised the necessity of acting with prudent caution in a matter of a nature so complex. An additional article to the Convention allowed a delay of five years for the entire abolition of the traffic.

It was farther stated in this paper, that the French Government was determined to pursue without relaxation the prosecution of the parties engaged in this barbarous traffic. Numerous condemnations had already taken place, and the tribunals had severely punished wherever the guilt of the accused was ascertained. The British memorandum stated that "it would be dreadful that the necessity of destroying human beings had become the consequence of that of concealing a traffic proscribed by the laws." This too just remark proved that the French law had been rigorously executed; and the cruel precautions taken by the violators of the treaty in order to secrete their victims proved, in a striking manner, the vigilance of the government.

In respect to one of the particular measures proposed by Great Britain, that of the introduction of a new public law declaring the offence of being engaged in the slave-trade to be piracy under the law of nations, the French plenipotentiaries declared, that "a deliberation tending to oblige all governments to apply to the slave-trade the punishment inflicted on the crime of piracy, could not, in their opinion, be within the province of a diplomatic conference."

In reply to this suggestion, the Duke of Wellington stated, in verbal conference, that his proposition had no other view than to engage all the maritime powers who had abolished the slave-trade to concert among themselves the measures to be adopted, in order to declare this traffic piracy, and to punish it accordingly.

M. de Chateaubriand rejoined, that the French plenipotentiaries had perfectly understood that the British memorandum required each government, separately, to pass a law assimilating the slave-trade to piracy; but that they could not sign a declaration in which this desire should be expressed, because they could not undertake to prescribe to their government the title, form, tenor, or extent of any laws.

The discussions at the Congress of Verona, thus resulted in a mere repetition of the barren denunciations of the Congress of Vienna and that of Aix-la-Chapelle. The three Northern powers of the Continent would not listen to the British proposition to grant a monopoly in their markets of the colonial products of such countries as had prohibited the slave-trade, nor to introduce a new public law of Europe by which the offence of engaging in the trade should be considered as piracy under the law of nations. France peremptorily refused to take any new measures to suppress the traffic.

Such is the account given of these transactions in the papers presented to the British Parliament. But we are told by M. de Chateaubriand, in his "History of the Congress of Verona," that in the memoir presented by the Duke of Wellington under date of the 24th November, 1822, the British cabinet expressed its regret that France should be the only one of the great maritime powers* which still refused to accede to the arrangements concluded between Great Britain and other States, with the view of conferring upon certain ships of war of the contracting parties the limited right of search and confiscation against merchant-vessels engaged in the slave-trade. M. de Chateaubriand answered this intimation by stating that the French Government could 'never consent to acknowledge the right of search. The national character, both of the French and English people, was opposed to its exercise, which, as between them, would be attended with the most fatal consequences; and if proofs were wanting in support of this opinion, they would be found in the fact that during that very year French blood had flowed on the coast of Africa. France recognised the freedom of the seas for all foreign flags to whatever lawful power they might belong : she only contended for that independence, in respect to herself, which she respected in others, and which was consistent with her national dignity.†

Great Britain could hardly expect to obtain from the Congress of Verona, at that period, this so much-coveted boon, nor any of the other concessions demanded in respect to a matter in which, though the interests of humanity were deeply concerned, the Continental powers perceived, that her colonial and commercial interests were also involved in the prosecution of the same cause. We

---

* It seems that Spain and Portugal were " great maritime powers," whilst Russia and the United States were not.

† Histoire du Congrès de Verone, tom. i.

say that Great Britain could hardly expect to obtain these concessions from the European Congress at that period, because she was strenuously opposed to the main object for which it had been assembled; that is to say, in order to countenance the armed interference of France in the internal affairs of Spain. The British cabinet had been gradually detaching itself, ever since the Congress of Troppau and that of Laybach, from the alliance between the great Continental powers, so far as that alliance was founded upon the claim of a general right to interfere in the internal transactions of other states, in order to prevent revolutionary changes in their forms of government or reigning dynasties.* This gradual separation from the Continental powers, on a point of policy so vitally important to them, begun by Lord Castlereagh (afterwards Marquess of Londonderry,) under the administration of the Earl of Liverpool, was continued and completed under that of Mr. Canning. Great Britain did not oppose by force, as the latter minister declared she might have done, the armed interference of France in the internal affairs of Spain; in consequence of which the constitution of the Cortes was overthrown, Ferdinand VII. restored to the plenitude of his royal authority, and British influence destroyed for a time in that part of the Peninsula. But she acknowledged the independence of the Spanish colonies on the American continent, and, as Mr. Can-

* See Lord Castlereagh's Circular Despatch of the 19th of January, 1821. (" British Annual Register," vol. lxii. pt. ii. p. 737.)

ning afterwards said, "called into existence a new world in order to redress the balance of the old."* This decisive measure, followed by the armed interference of Great Britain in the internal affairs of Portugal in 1826, disturbed the intimacy of her relations with the great Powers of the Continent, and rendered them still less disposed to yield any point of peculiar interest to her without adequate equivalents. This unaccommodating disposition continued, as we shall hereafter see, until the French revolution of 1830, by separating for a time France under her new dynasty of the house of Orleans, from the general European alliance, enabled Great Britain to obtain from that power the concession of the right of search, which was yielded to the influence of those philanthropic sentiments and unsuspecting confidence in British friendship which marked that era. The treaty of the 15th July, 1840, relating to the affairs of the Levant, once more attracted Great Britain within the sphere of the influence of the Northern powers; and prepared the way for the treaty of the 20th of December, 1841, by which the right of search was at last conceded by those powers who had been formerly the great champions of neutral maritime rights. By what circumstances France was induced to accede to this compact, it would be beside our purpose to inquire.

In the mean time the slave-trade continued to

---

* Mr. Canning's Speech in the House of Commons on the British armed intervention in the affairs of Portugal, 11th December. 1826. ("British Annual Register," vol. lxviii. p. 192.)

be carried on to an enormous extent, and with circumstances of cruelty augmented by the very measures adopted for its suppression. This notorious fact is attested by the British diplomatic correspondence upon this subject, by the Reports of the African Institution in London, and by those made from the committees of the American Congress and British Parliament. No little proportion of this traffic in human flesh and blood was carried on under the Spanish and Portuguese flags with British capital, on British account, and in vessels built in London and Liverpool.* The trade had been nominally prohibited by Spain to her subjects from the 31st of May, 1820, on all parts of the African coast, both south and north of the equinoctial line; but Portugal still continued to cling to that portion she had reserved south of the equator. In 1821, there was not a single flag of any European state that could lawfully cover the traffic to the north of the equator; yet down to the year 1830, and we may add down to the present time, the fraudulent importation of African slaves actually continued, if it was not openly countenanced, from the Rio de la Plata to the Amazon, and throughout the whole West Indian archipelago.† The com-

* In the debate in the House of Commons on the 9th February, 1818, Lord Castlereagh said, " It would be a great error to believe that the reproach of carrying on the slave-trade illegally belonged only to the other countries. In numberless instances, he was sorry to say, it had come to his knowledge that British subjects were indirectly and largely engaged."

† Report of the House of Representatives in the American Congress, 16th February, 1825.

mercial cupidity of individuals, the financial and political interests of States, and the inveterate habits of ages, by which Africa has been condemned to barbarism from the earliest records of history, were too powerful to be overcome by the mere operation of laws and treaties, aided by the zealous efforts of benevolent individuals and associations, within the short compass of a few brief years. "MAN," says Sir Thomas Fowell Buxton, "has ever been the great staple article of exportation from Africa, by which chiefly her inhabitants have acquired the luxuries of civilized life." That most zealous, constant, and enlightened advocate of the slave-trade abolition has recently retired from the contest in disgust and despair (so far as the means hitherto pursued for its execution are concerned;) after having conclusively shown that what was true in 1830 remains true to this day, and that no actual progress has been made in the suppression of the traffic, which, on the contrary, has rapidly increased since the abolition, both in the numbers of its victims and the sum total of their sufferings.\* This

---

\* Sir T. F. Buxton, in his recent "History of the Abolition of the Slave-Trade," has, in our opinion, established, from conclusive testimony and fair deductions, that more than 150,000 negroes are now transported across the ocean from the eastern and western coasts of Africa;\* that the arms and other articles peculiarly adapted to the slave-trade are still manufactured on the most extensive scale in Great Britain; that the mortality of the middle

---

\* Whilst Mr. Pitt and Mr. Fox computed the numbers carried over in 1792 at only 80,000.

should not, perhaps, discourage more ardent and energetic partisans of the measure, if any such there be ; but, at least, it should render them cautious in selecting the means by which they would seek to attain an object which has hitherto eluded their grasp, and, like the mirage of the African desert, fled before them as they seemed to approach its borders.   But above all, they should take care

passage is frightfully augmented by the very precautions which are rendered necessary to escape from the vigilance of the cruisers: and whilst double the number of human victims are sacrificed to this accursed traffic than at the time when Clarkson and Wilberforce began their philanthropic labours, each individual suffers tenfold more from the contracted space in which they are stowed, every thing being sacrificed to fast sailing.   He considers the measure of abolition as having totally failed, not for want of energy and perseverance in its execution, but from a total mistake as to the true means of accomplishing the object.   His opinion is that Great Britain will never be able to obtain the assent of *all* nations to the exercise of the right of search for this object; and even if she did obtain the assent of all, the advantage would be illusory. That even if to this concession were superadded the introduction of a new public law, by which the traffic should be denounced and punished as piracy under the law of nations, it would be all in vain; the enormous profits (more than fifteen per cent) made by it affording a premium which counteracts every precaution which can possibly be taken to execute the prohibitory laws and treaties. He, therefore, concludes that the trade will never be destroyed by the means heretofore devised.   The African, until civilized, will never cease to desire arms, ardent spirits, and other luxuries, nor to purchase them in exchange for men, which have ever been the great staple article of exportation from that continent.   The true means of repression to be adopted are to civilize, and Christianize, and colonize Africa, by which the native chieftains would cease to have an interest in dealing in human flesh.

that among these means be not included an invasion of the sovereign rights of foreign states, as independent of Great Britain as Great Britain is of
them. They should remember that their greatest
civilian has said, speaking of this very subject, that
"no one nation has a right to force the way to the
liberation of Africa by trampling on the independence of other states; or to procure an eminent
good by means that are unlawful; or to press forward to a great principle by breaking through other
principles that stand in the way."*

We have already observed that so long as the
European war continued, the British laws, abolishing the slave-trade as to their own subjects, were
executed by means of the belligerent right of visitation and search, so far as the neutral flag was used
to cover the illicit traffic still carried on with British
capital and on British account. Vessels captured
and brought in for adjudication under the exercise
of this right, though they might not prove to belong
to an enemy, were condemned, according to the well-
known fiction and formula of the Prize Courts, *as
enemy's property*, in case of proof that they had
fraudulently assumed the neutral flag in order to
cover British interests in a traffic interdicted by the
British Parliament to those who were amenable to
its laws. On principle, it would seem that the belligerent right of capture and condemnation in this

* See the judgment of Sir William Scott (since Lord Stowell)
in the case of the French slave-trade ship le Louis (Dodson's
"Admiralty Reports," vol. ii. p. 238.)

respect could not be carried farther than thus incidentally to execute the municipal statutes of the belligerent state, by rejecting the claim of a subject of that state, whose property should be taken in violating its revenue laws, or laws of trade, and brought in for adjudication in the Admiralty Courts of his own country. But a case occurred in 1810, in which the doctrine was carried much farther, and extended to property belonging to a *neutral* state, and taken in the act of violating the municipal laws of the owner's country. Such was the case of the Amadie, an American vessel employed in transporting slaves from the coast of Africa to a Spanish-American colony. The vessel was captured, with the slaves on board, by a British cruiser; and the vessel and cargo condemned to the use of the captors in the Vice-Admiralty Court at Tortola. On appeal to the Lords of Appeal in Prize and Plantation Causes, the sentence was affirmed. The judgment of the appellant Court was delivered by Sir William Grant in the following terms:—

"This ship must be considered as being employed, at the time of capture, in carrying slaves from the coast of Africa to a Spanish colony. We think that this was evidently the original plan and purpose of the voyage, notwithstanding the pretence set up to veil the true intention. The claimant, however, who is an American, complains of the capture, and demands from us the restitution of property of which he alleges that he has been unjustly dispossessed. In all the former cases of this kind which have come before this Court, the slave-trade was liable to considerations very different from those which belong to it now. It had, at that time, been prohibited (so far as respected carrying slaves to the colonies of foreign nations) by America, but by our own laws it was still allowed. It appeared to us, therefore, difficult to consider the prohibitory law of America in any other light than as one of those municipal regulations of a foreign state of which this Court could not take any cognizance. But by the alteration which has since taken place, the question stands on different grounds, and is open to the application of very different principles. The slave-trade has since been totally abolished by this country, and our legislature has pronounced it to be contrary to the principles of justice and humanity. Whatever we might think as individuals before, we could not, sitting as judges in a British court of justice, regard the trade in that light while our own laws permitted it. But we can now assert that this trade cannot, abstractedly speaking, have a legitimate existence.

" When I say *abstractedly speaking*, I mean that this country has no right to control any foreign legislature that may think fit to dissent from this doctrine, and to permit to its own subjects the prosecution of this trade; but we have a right to affirm that *primâ facie* the trade is illegal, and thus to throw on claimants the burden of proof that in respect of them, by the authority of their own laws, it is otherwise. As the case now stands, we think we are entitled to say that a claimant can have no right, upon principles of universal law, to claim the restitution in a Prize Court of human beings carried as slaves. He must show some right that has been violated by the capture, some property of which he has been dispossessed to which he ought to be restored. In this case the laws of the claimant's country allow of no property such as he claims. There can, therefore, be no right to restitution. The consequence is that the judgment must be affirmed."*

It may seem amazing that such a judicial mind as that of Sir William Grant, at once acute and discriminating, whose clear judgment was not likely to be disturbed by passionate sympathy in the cause of abolition should have arrived at such a conclusion from such premises. What a rapid stride must public opinion have taken in England, since the time when she extorted from Spain at the peace of Utrecht the Assiento contract, securing the monopoly of the slave-trade with the Spanish colonies, "as the whole price of the victories of Ramillies and Blenheim;" when she "higgled at Aix-la-Chapelle for four years longer of this exclusive trade;" when "in the treaty of Madrid, she clung to the last remains of the Assiento contract;" and, to come nearer the moment this anomalous judgment was pronounced, when Lord Eldon, opposing the abolition as the leader of the court-party in Parliament in 1807, entered into a review of the measures adopted by England respecting the trade, which, he contended, " Had been sanctioned by par-

* Acton's " Admiralty Reports," vol. i. p. 240.—Fifth Report of the Directors of the African Institution, pp. 11, 13.

liaments in which sat the wisest lawyers, the most learned divines, and the most excellent statesmen;" when Lord Hawksbury (afterwards Earl of Liverpool) moved that the words, "inconsistent with the principles of justice and humanity," should be struck out of the preamble to the Slave-trade Abolition-Bill; when the Earl of Westmoreland declared that, "Though he should see the Presbyterian and the prelate, the Methodist and field-preacher, the Jacobin and murderer, unite in favour of the measure of abolition, he would raise his voice against it in parliament!"*—what a rapid stride, we repeat, must public opinion have taken in England in the brief interval between these speeches in the House of Lords and the delivery of the above judgment at the Cock-pit, for such a self-balanced mind as that of Sir William Grant to be thrown from its centre by the abstractions which form the basis of his judgment, and by which the high Court in which he presided was induced to usurp the illegitimate power of executing the penal laws of another independent country!

In the case of the Fortuna, determined in 1811, in the High Court of Admiralty, on appeal from the inferior court, Lord Stowell, with evident reluctance and against the manifest convictions of his own superior mind, condemned another American vessel with her cargo as destined to be employed in the African slave-trade. In delivering his judgment in this case, he stated, that an Ameri-

* Hansard's "Parliamentary Debates," vol. viii.

can ship, *quasi* American, was entitled, upon proof, to immediate restitution; but she might forfeit, as other neutral ships might, that title, by various acts of misconduct, by violations of belligerent rights most clearly and universally. But though the Prize-Court looked primarily to violations of belligerent rights as grounds of confiscation in vessels not actually belonging to the enemy, it had extended itself a good deal beyond considerations of that description only. It had been established by recent decisions of the Supreme Court, that the Court of Prize, though properly a court purely of the law of nations, has a right to notice the municipal law of this country *in the case of a British vessel* which, in the course of a prize-proceeding, appears to have been trading in violation of that law, and to reject a claim for her on that account. That principle had been incorporated into the prize-law of this country within the last twenty years, and seemed now fully incorporated. A late decision in the case of the Amadie seemed to have gone the length of establishing a principle, that any trade contrary to the general law of nations, although not tending to, or accompanied with, any infraction of the law of that country whose tribunals were called upon to consider it, might subject the vessels employed in that trade to confiscation. The Amadie was an American ship employed in carrying on the slave-trade; a trade which this country, *since its own abandonment of it,* had deemed repugnant to the law of nations, to justice, and humanity; though without presuming so to consider and treat it where it occurs in the practice of the subjects of a state which continued to tolerate and protect it by its own municipal regulations : but it put upon the parties the burden of showing that it was so tolerated and protected; and in failure of producing such proof, proceeded to condemnation, as it did in the case of that vessel. " How far that judgment has been universally concurred in and approved," continued Lord Stowell, " is not for me to inquire. *If there be those who disapprove of it, I certainly am not at liberty to include myself in that number, because the decisions of that Court bind authoritatively the conscience of this;* its decisions must be conformed to, *and its principles practically adopted.* The principle laid down in that case appears to be, that the slave-trade carried on by a vessel belonging to a subject of the United States is a trade which, being unprotected by the domestic regulations of their legislature and government, subjects the vessel engaged in it to a sentence of condemnation. If the ship should therefore turn out to be an American, actually employed; it matters not, in my opinion, in what stage of the employment, whether in the inception, or the prosecution, or the consummation of it; the case of the Amadie will bind the conscience of this Court to the effect of compelling it to pronounce a sentence of confiscation."*

In a subsequent case, that of the Diana, Lord Stowell limited the application of the doctrine in-

* Dodson's " Admiralty Reports," vol. i. p. 81.   Fifth Report of the Committee of the African Institution, p. 15.

vented by Sir W. Grant to the special circumstances which distinguished the case of the Amadie. The Diana was a Swedish vessel, captured by a British cruiser on the coast of Africa whilst actually engaged in carrying slaves to the Swedish West India possessions. The vessel and cargo was restored to the Swedish owner, on the ground that Sweden had not then prohibited the trade, by law or convention, and still continued to tolerate it in practice. It was stated by Lord Stowell, in delivering the judgment of the High Court of Admiralty in this case, that England had abolished the trade as unjust and criminal ; but she claimed no right of enforcing that prohibition against the subjects of those states which had not adopted the same opinion; and England did not mean to set herself up as the legislator and *custos morum* for the whole world, or presume to interfere with the commercial regulations of other states. The principle of the case of the Amadie was, that where the municipal law of the country to which the parties belonged had prohibited the trade, British tribunals would hold it to be illegal, upon general principles of justice and humanity ; but they would respect the property of persons engaged in it under the sanction of the laws of their own country.*

The above three cases arose during the continuance of the war, and whilst the laws and treaties prohibiting the slave-trade were incidentally exe-

* Dodson's " Admiralty Reports," vol. i. p. 95.

cuted through the exercise of the belligerent right of visitation and search.

In the case of the Diana, Lord Stowell had sought to distinguish the circumstances of that case from those of the Amadie, so as to raise a distinction between the case of the subjects of a country which had already prohibited the slave-trade from that of those whose government still continued to tolerate it. At last came the case of the French vessel called the Louis, captured after the general peace by a British cruiser, and condemned in the inferior Court of Admiralty. Lord Stowell reversed the sentence in 1817, discarding altogether the authority of the Amadie as a precedent, both upon general reasoning which went to shake that case to its very foundations, and upon the special ground, that even admitting that the trade had been actually prohibited by the municipal laws of France (which was doubtful,) the right of visitation and search (being an exclusively belligerent right,) could not consistently with the law of nations be exercised in time of peace to enforce that prohibition by the British courts upon the property of French subjects. In delivering the judgment of the High Court of Admiralty in this case, Lord Stowell held that the slave-trade, though unjust and condemned by the statute-law of England was not piracy, nor was it a crime by the universal law of nations. A court of justice, in the administration of law, must look to the legal standard of morality,—a standard which, upon a question of this nature, must be found in

thé law of nations as fixed and evidenced by general, ancient, and admitted practice, by treaties, and
by the general tenor of the laws, ordinances, and
formal transactions of civilized states; and looking
to these authorities, he found a difficulty in maintaining that the transaction was legally criminal.
To make it piracy or a crime by the universal law
of nations, it must have been so considered and
treated in practice by all civilized states, or made so
by virtue of a general convention.

The slave-trade, on the contrary, had been carried
on by all nations, including Great Britain, until
a very recent period, and was still carried on by
Spain and Portugal, and not yet entirely prohibited
by France. It was not, therefore, a criminal
traffic by the consuetudinary law of nations ; and
every nation, independently of special compact,
retained a legal right to carry it on. No nation
could exercise the right of visitation and search upon
the common and unappropriated parts of the ocean
except upon the belligerent claim. No one nation
had a right to force its way to the liberation of
Africa by trampling on the independence of other
states ; or to procure an eminent good by means
that are unlawful ; or to press forward to a great
principle by breaking through other great principles that stand in the way. The right of visitation
and search on the high seas did not exist in time of
peace. If it belonged to one nation, it equally
belonged to all, and would lead to gigantic mischief
and universal war. Other nations had refused to
accede to the British proposal of a reciprocal right

of search in the African seas, and it would require
an express convention to give the right of search in
time of peace.*

The leading principles of this judgment were
confirmed in 1820 by the Court of King's Bench,
in the case of *Madrazo* v. *Willis*, in which the
point of the illegality of the slave-trade under the
general law of nations came incidentally in question.
The Court held that the British statutes against the
slave-trade were applicable to British subjects only.
The British Parliament could not prevent the subjects of other states from carrying on the trade out
of the limits of the British dominions. If a ship be
acting contrary to the general law of nations, she is
thereby subject to condemnation; but it was impossible to say that the slave-trade is contrary to
the law of nations. It was, until lately, carried on
by all the nations of Europe; and a practice so
sanctioned could only be rendered illegal, on the
principles of international law, by the consent of
all the powers. Many states had so consented, but
others had not; and the adjudged cases had gone no
farther that to establish the rule, that ships belonging to countries that had prohibited the trade were
liable to capture and condemnation, if found engaged
in it.†

A similar course of reasoning was adopted by the
Supreme Court of the United States in 1825, in the
case of Spanish and Portuguese vessels engaged in
the slave-trade, whilst that trade was still tolerated by

* Dodson's "Admiralty Reports," vol. ii. p. 210.
† Barnwell's and Alderson's "Reports," vol. iii. p. 353.

the laws of Spain and Portugal, captured by American cruisers, and brought in for adjudication in the Admiralty Courts of the Union. In delivering the judgment of the Supreme Court in one of these cases, Mr. Chief-Justice Marshall stated that it could hardly be denied that the slave-trade was contrary to the law of nature; that every man had a natural right to the fruits of his own labour was generally admitted; and that no other person could rightly deprive him of those fruits, and appropriate them against his will, seemed to be the necessary result of this admission. But from the earliest times war had existed, and war conferred rights in which all had acquiesced. Among the most enlightened nations of antiquity, one of these rights was, that the victor might enslave the vanquished. That which was the usage of all nations could not be pronounced repugnant to the law of nations, which was certainly to be tried by the test of general usage. That which had received the assent of all must be the law of all.

Slavery, then, had its origin in force; but as the world had agreed that it was a legitimate result of force, the state of things which was thus produced by general consent could not be pronounced unlawful.

Throughout Christendom this harsh rule had been exploded, and war was no longer considered as giving a right to enslave captures. But this triumph had not been universal. The parties to the modern law of nations do not propagate their principles by force; and Africa had not yet adopted them

Throughout the whole extent of that immense continent, so far as we know its history, it is still the law of nations that prisoners are slaves. The question then was, could those who had renounced this law be permitted to participate in its effects, by purchasing the human beings who are its victims?

Whatever might be the answer of a moralist to this question, a jurist must search for its legal solution in those principles which are sanctioned by the usages,—the national acts and the general assent of that portion of the world, of which he considers himself a part, and to whose law the appeal is made. If we resort to this standard as the test of international law, the question must be considered as decided in favour of the legality of the trade. Both Europe and America embarked in it; and for nearly two centuries it was carried on without opposition and without censure. A jurist could not say that a practice thus supported was illegal, and that those engaged in it might be punished, either personally or by deprivation of property.

In this commerce, thus sanctioned by universal consent, every nation had an equal right to engage. No principle of general law was more universally acknowledged than the perfect equality of nations. Russia and Geneva have equal rights. It results from this equality, that no one can rightfully impose a rule on another. Each legislates for itself, but its legislation can operate on itself alone. A right, then, which was vested in all by the consent of all, could be divested only by consent; and this trade, in which all had participated, must remain lawful to those who could not be induced to relinquish it. As no nation could prescribe a rule for others, no one could make a law of nations; and this traffic remained lawful to those whose government had not forbidden it.

If it was consistent with the laws of nations, it could not in itself be piracy: it could be made so only by statute; and the obligation of the statute could not transcend the legislative power of the state which might enact it.

If the trade was neither repugnant to the law of nations nor piratical, it was almost superfluous to say in that Court that the right of bringing in for adjudication in time of peace, even where the vessel belonged to a nation which had prohibited the trade, could not exist. The courts of justice of no country executed the penal laws of another; and the course of policy of the American Government on the subject of visitation and search would decide any case against the captors in which that right had been exercised by an American cruiser, on the vessels of a foreign nation not violating the municipal laws of the United States. It followed, that a foreign vessel engaged in the African slave-trade, captured on the high seas in time of peace by an American cruiser, and brought in for adjudication, would be restored to the original owners.*

We thus perceive that the highest judicial authorities in both countries concur in declaring that the African slave-trade is not prohibited by the general

---

* Wheaton's "Reports," vol. x. p. 66. The Antelope.

law of nations; and that so far as prohibited by the municipal laws of particular states, or by special compacts between particular states, such prohibition can only be enforced by the tribunals of that country in which it has been enacted, or, in the other alternative, of such countries as are parties to the compact. That if the slave-trade be not unlawful by the general law of nations, still less can it be considered as piracy under that law, to be punished as such in a court of the law of nations. That the right of visitation and search on the high seas by the armed and commissioned vessels of one nation upon the merchant-vessels of another, does not exist in time of peace, unless by special compact, binding only on those who have freely consented to become parties to such compact. And that, consequently, the right of visitation and search cannot be thus exercised in time of peace, for the purpose of bringing in for adjudication the vessels of any nation suspected of being engaged in the slave-trade, whether the trade has been prohibited by the municipal laws of that nation or not, unless it has expressly consented to the exercise of the right for that purpose.

Such was the state of judicial opinion in England respecting the legality of the slave-trade according to the recognised principle of public law, when a joint address of the two Houses of Parliament was presented to the Prince Regent on the 9th of July, 1819, congratulating his Royal Highness upon the success which had crowned the efforts of the British Government for the suppression of the slave-trade; that guilty traffic having been declared by the concurrent voice of all the great powers of Europe, assembled in Congress, to be repugnant to the principle of humanity and of universal morality.

That, consequently, on this declaration, all the states whose subjects were formerly concerned in this criminal traffic had since prohibited it, the greater part absolutely and entirely; some, for a time, partially, on that part of the coast of Africa only which is to the north of the line: of the two states (Spain and Portugal) which still tolerated the traffic, one would soon cease to be thus distinguished; the period which Spain had fixed for the total abolition of the trade being near at hand: one power alone (Portugal) had hitherto forborne to specify any period when the traffic should be absolutely prohibited.

That the United States of America were honourably distinguished *as the first which pronounced the condemnation of the guilty traffic;* and that they had since successively passed various laws for carrying their prohibition into effect:

That, nevertheless, the two Houses of Parliament could not but hear with feelings of deep regret, that, notwithstanding the strong condemnation of the crime by all the great powers of Europe and by the United States of America, there was reason to fear that the measures which had been hitherto adopted for actually suppressing these crimes were not yet adequate to their purpose:

That they never, however, could admit the persuasion that so great and generous a people as that of France, which had condemned this guilty commerce in the strongest terms, would be less earnest than the British nation to wipe away so foul a blot on the character of a Christian people:

That they, if possible, were still less willing to admit such a supposition in the instance of the United States; a people derived originally from the same common stock with the British nation, and favoured, like them, in a degree hitherto perhaps unequalled in the history of the world, with the enjoyment of civil and religious liberty, and all their attendant blessings:

"That the consciousness *that the Government of this country was originally instrumental in leading the Americans into this criminal course,* must naturally prompt us to call on them the more importunately to join us in endeavouring to put an entire end to the evil of which it is productive."

The Address farther stated that the two Houses of Parliament conceived that the establishment of some concert and co-operation in the measures to be taken by the different powers for the execution of their common purpose, might, in various respects, be of great practical utility; and that under the impression of this persuasion, several of the European states had already entered into conventional arrangements for seizing vessels engaged in the criminal traffic, and for bringing to punishment those who should still be guilty of these nefarious practices:

That they, therefore, supplicated his Royal Highness to renew his beneficent endeavours, more especially with the Governments of France and of the United States of America, for the effectual attainment of an object which all professed equally to have in view; and they could not but indulge the confident hope that their efforts might yet, ere long, produce their desired effect,—might ensure the practical enforcement of principles universally acknowledged to be undeniably just and true,—and might obtain for the long afflicted people of Africa the actual termination of their wrongs and miseries,—and might destroy for ever that fatal barrier which, by obstructing the ordinary course of civilization and social improvement, had so long kept a large portion of the globe in darkness and barbarism, and rendered its connexion with the civilized and Christian nations of the earth a fruitful source only of wretchedness and desolation.*

Sustained with the support given by this Parliamentary Address, Lord Castlereagh once more renewed the efforts he had previously made to secure the assent of the American Government to the exercise of the right of visitation and search in time of peace as a means of more effectually suppressing the slave-trade.

In consequence of his lordship's instructions, Sir Stratford Canning, the British minister at Washington, presented to Mr. John Quincy Adams, Secretary of State of the American Government, a note, under date of 20th of December, 1820, stating that notwithstanding all that had been done on both sides of the Atlantic for the suppression of the African slave-trade, it was notorious that an

* Fourteenth Report of the African Institution, pp. 4–7.

illicit commerce, attended with aggravating suffer-
ing to its unhappy victims, was still carried on;
and that it was generally acknowledged that a combined system of maritime police could alone afford
the means of putting it down with effect.

The note farther stated, that the concurrence of
principle in the condemnation and prohibition of
the slave-trade, which had so honourably distinguished the British Parliament and American Congress, seemed naturally and unavoidably to lead to
a concert of measures between the two governments,
the moment such co-operation was recognised as
necessary for the accomplishment of their mutual
purpose. It could not be anticipated that either of
the parties, discouraged by such difficulties as are
inseparable from all human transactions of any
magnitude, would be content to acquiesce in the
continuance of a practice so flagrantly immoral,
especially at the (then) present favourable period,
when the slave-trade was completely prohibited to
the north of the equator and countenanced by Portugal alone to the south of that line.

The note concluded by stating, that Mr. Adams
was fully acquainted with the particular measures
recommended by His Majesty's ministers as best
calculated, in their opinion, to attain the object
which both parties had in view; but he need not be
reminded that the British Government was too sincere in the pursuit of that common object to press
the adoption of its own proposal, however satisfactory in themselves, to the exclusion of any sugges-
tions equally conducive to the same end, and more

agreeable to the institutions or prevailing opinions of other nations.

In his reply to this note, Mr. Adams stated, that the proposals made by the British Government to the United States, inviting their accession to the arrangements contained in the treaties relating to the slave-trade with Spain, Portugal, and the Netherlands, to which Great Britain was a reciprocal contracting party, had been again taken into consideration by the President, with an anxious desire of contributing to the final suppression of the trade to the utmost extent of the powers within the competency of the Federal Government, and by means compatible with its duties in respect to the rights of its own citizens and the principles of its national independence.

The reply farther stated, that at an earlier period of the communications between the two governments upon this subject, the President, in manifesting his sensibility to the amicable spirit of confidence with which the measures concerted between Great Britain and some of her European allies had been made known to the United States, and to the candid offer of admitting them to a participation in those measures, had instructed the American minister in London to represent the difficulties which placed the President under the necessity of declining the proposal. These difficulties resulted, as well from *certain principles of international law of the deepest and most painful interest to the United States,* as from limitations of authority prescribed by the American people to the legislative and executive depositories of the national power. On this occasion it had been represented, that a compact, giving the power to the naval officers of one nation to search the merchant-vessels of another for offenders and offences against the latter, backed by a farther power to seize and carry into a foreign port, and there subject to the decision of a tribunal composed of, at least, one-half foreigners, irresponsible to the supreme corrective tribunal of the American Union, and not amenable to the control of impeachment for official misdemeanour, was an investment of power over the persons, property, and reputation of the citizens of that country, not only unwarranted by any delegation of sovereign power to the national government, but so adverse to the elementary principles and indispensable securities interwoven in all the political institutions of the United States, that not even the most unqualified approbation of the ends to which the proposed organization of authority was adopted, nor the most sincere and earnest wish to concur in every suitable expedient for their accomplishment, could reconcile it to those sentiments and principles of which, in the estimation of the American people and government, no consideration whatever could justify the transgression.

Mr. Adams also referred, in his reply to the note of Sir Stratford Canning, to several conferences between them, in which the subject had been fully and freely discussed, and in which the incompetency of the power of the American Government to become a party to the institution of tribunals organized like those stipulated in the treaties above noticed, and the incompatibility of such tribunals with the constitutional rights guaranteed to every citizen of the Union, had been shown by references to the fundamental principles of the American Government, by which the supreme, unlimited, sovereign power is considered as inherent in the whole body of the people, whilst its delegations are limited and restricted by the terms of the instruments sanctioned by them, under which the powers of legislation, judgment, and execution, are administered, and by special indications of those articles in the constitution of the United States which expressly prohibit their constituted authorities from erecting any judicial courts, by the forms of the process belonging to which American citizens should be called to answer for any penal offence without the intervention of a grand jury to accuse and of a jury of trial to decide upon the charge.

But, while regretting that the character of the organized means of co-operation for the suppression of the African slave-trade proposed by Great Britain did not admit of the President's concurrence in the adoption of them, he had been far from the disposition to reject or discountenance the general proposition of concerted co-operation with Great Britain to the accomplishment of the common end—the suppression of the slave-trade. For this purpose, armed cruisers of the United States had been for some time kept stationed on that coast which was the scene of this odious traffic,—a measure which the American Government intended to continue without intermission. As there were armed British vessels charged with the same duty, Mr. Adams was directed by the President to propose that instructions, to be concerted between the two governments, with a view to mutual assistance, should be given to the commanders of the vessels respectively assigned to that service; that they should be ordered, whenever convenient, to cruise in company together, to communicate mutually all information which might be useful to the execution of their respective duties, and to give each other every assistance compatible with their own service and adapted to the end which was the common object of both parties.

These measures, it was added, congenial to the spirit which had so long and so steadily marked the policy of the United States in the vindication of the rights of humanity, would, it was hoped, prove effectual to the purposes for which their co-operation was desired by the British Government, and to which the American Union would continue to direct its most strenuous and persevering exertions.

In a despatch from Lord Castlereagh to Sir Stratford Canning, dated the 25th of March, 1821, the former expressed his disappointment that the counter proposal of the American Government fell so far short of the object which the British Government had in view; but Sir Stratford Canning was instructed to communicate to the American Government the instructions under which the British naval force stationed in the African seas was acting, and to inform it that additional instructions would immediately be sent to the British vessels engaged in that service to co-operate with such American vessels as might be employed in those seas for the extinction of the traffic.*

It appears, then, that the American Government still adhered, in 1820–21, to their original objections to the concession of the right of visitation and search as demanded by the British Government.

On the 29th of January, 1823, Sir Stratford Canning once more addressed an official letter on this subject to Mr. Adams, stating that the British Government still remained convinced that the only effectual means of suppressing the traffic was to be found in the proposed mutual concession of the right of search. He, at the same time, invited the communication on the part of the American Government of some efficient counter proposal originating with itself. The letter also requested the American cabinet to give instructions to its envoy at Paris to concur with the British ambassador in a joint representation to the French Government on the subject of the slave-trade, which still continued to be carried on under the French flag.

On the 8th of March, 1823, a resolution passed the House of Representatives, " That the President of the United States be requested to enter upon, and to prosecute, from time to time, such negotiations with the several maritime powers of Europe and America, as he may deem expedient, for the effectual abolition of the African slave-trade and its

* Supplement to the Annual Report of the Directors of the African Institution for the year 1821, pp. 151–157.

ultimate denunciation as piracy, under the law of nations, by the consent of the civilized world."

On the 31st March, 1823, Mr. Adams replied to Sir S. Canning's letter, stating that the answer had been delayed, not by any abatement of the interest felt by the American Government for the final suppression of the slave-trade, nor by any hesitation as to persevering in its former refusal to submit their vessels and citizens to the search of foreign officers upon the high seas, but by an expectation that the proceedings in Congress would indicate to the executive government views upon which it might be enabled to substitute a proposal more effectual for this purpose and less objectionable than that to which the United States could not be reconciled, namely, that of granting the right of search. These proceedings had resulted in the above resolution, which would doubtless have obtained the sanction of the senate, had there been time to collect the opinion of that branch of the national legislation before the close of the cession. The President had, therefore, no hesitation in acting upon the expressed and almost unanimous sense of the House of Representatives, so far as to declare the willingness of the American Union to join with other nations in the common engagement to pursue and punish those who shall continue to practise this crime, so reprobated by the just and humane of every country as enemies of the human race, and to fix them, irrevocably, in the class and under the denomination of pirates.

Mr. Adams also transmitted to Sir S. Canning a copy of the act of Congress of the 15th May, 1820, by which any citizen of the United States, being of the crew of any *foreign* ship engaged in the slave-trade, or *any* person whatever being of the crew of any ship owned, in whole or in part, or navigated in behalf of American citizens, participating in the slave-trade, is declared to have incurred the penalties of piracy, and made liable to atone for the crime with his life. The legislature of a single nation could go no farther to mark its abhorrence of this traffic, or to deter the people subject to its laws from contamination by the practices of others.

Mr. Adams farther stated that if, as represented by Sir S. Canning, the French flag was more particularly employed to cover the illicit trade on the coast of Africa, and to conceal the property and persons of individuals bound to other allegiances, the act of Congress above mentioned made every American citizen concerned in such covered trade liable, when detected, to suffer an ignominious death. The code of Great Britain herself had hitherto provided no provision of equal severity in the prosecution of her subjects, even under the shelter of foreign flags and the covert of simulated papers and property.

Mr. Adams concluded by stating that he was instructed by the President to propose the adoption by Great Britain of the *principles* of this act, and to offer a mutual stipulation to annex the penalties of piracy to the offence of participating in the slave-trade by the citizens or subjects of the two countries. This proposal was made as a substitute for that of conceding the mutual right of search, and of a trial by mixed commissions, which would be rendered useless by it. Should it meet the approbation of the

British Government, it might be separately urged
upon the adoption of France and the other European
powers in the manner most conducive to its ultimate
success.

This counter-proposal, which had been invited by
the intimation in Sir S. Canning's letter, calling for
a substitute to the British proposal of a mutual concession of the right of search, was received by him
in the most ungracious manner.   Instead of answer-
ing the American counter-proposal, he proceeded,
in his letter of the 8th of April, 1823, to discuss the
original British proposal for the concession of a reciprocal right of search, and endeavoured to obviate
the various objections which had induced the American Government peremptorily to reject that proposal.   He at the same time intimated that the captured vessels, instead of being tried before a mixed
commission might be carried in for adjudication before the ordinary Courts of Admiralty of the captor's
country, or before the similar courts of that country
to which the captured vessels belonged.   This intimation, he conceived, would remove the constitutional objections previously urged by the American
cabinet against the proposed mixed commissions.
But the first part only of this alternative was distinctly proposed by the British negotiator, and was
considered by Mr. Adams in his reply as wholly inadmissible.

In his reply, dated the 24th June, 1823, the
American Secretary of State observed, that his
offer was presented as a substitute for that of conceding a mutual right of search with a trial by

mixed commissions, to which the United States could not be reconciled, and which would be rendered useless by the proposed substitute.

Sir S. Canning, in his letter of the 8th April, had intimated that the British Government would be disposed to receive this offer only as an acknowledgment that measures, more efficient than any then generally in force, were indispensable for the suppression of the slave-trade ; and although it had never opposed the consideration of another plan brought forward as equally effective, yet having from the first regarded a mutual concession of the right of search as the *only* true and practical cure for the evil, their prevailing sentiment would be that of regret at the unfavourable view still taken of it by the American Government. Sir S. Canning's letter therefore urged a reconsideration of it, and by presenting important modifications, of the proposal heretofore made, removed some of the objections taken to it as insuperable, whilst it offered argumentative answers to the others which had been disclosed in the previous correspondence.

In the treaties concluded by Great Britain with Spain, Portugal, and the Netherlands, for the suppression of the slave-trade, and communicated to the American Government with an invitation to enter into similar engagements, three principles were involved, to neither of which that government felt itself at liberty to accede.

The 1st was the mutual concession of the right of search and capture, in time of peace, over merchant-vessels on the coast of Africa. The 2d was the exercise of that right even over vessels sailing under convoy of the public officers of their own nations; and the 3d was the trial of the captured vessels by mixed commissions in colonial settlements, under no subordination to the ordinary judicial tribunals of the country to which the party brought before them should belong.

In Sir S. Canning's letter of the 8th of April, an *expectation* was authorized that an arrangement for the adjudication of the vessels detained might leave them to be disposed of in the ordinary way, by the sentence of an Admiralty Court in the captor's country, or place them under the jurisdiction of a similar court in the country to which they belonged; to the former alternative of which the British envoy anticipated the ready assent of the United States, in consequence of the aggravated nature of the crime as acknowledged by their laws, which would thus be " submitted to the jurisdiction of a *foreign* Court of Admiralty." But it was precisely because it was *foreign*, that the objection was taken to the trial by mixed commissions; and if it transcended the constitutional authority of the United States' government to subject the persons, property, and reputations of their citizens to the decisions of a court partly composed of their own countrymen, it might seem needless to remark that the constitutional objection could not diminish, in proportion as its cause should increase, or that the power competent to make American citizens amenable to a court consisting of one-half foreigners, should be adequate to place their liberty, their fortune, and their fame at the disposal of tribunals *entirely foreign.*

Mr. Adams farther remarked that the sentence of an Admiralty Court in the country of the captor was not the *ordinary* way by which the vessels of one nation, taken on the high seas by the officers of another, are tried in time of peace. There was in the ordinary way no right whatever existing to take, to search, or even to board them; and he took that occasion to express the great satisfaction with which the American Government had seen this principle solemnly recognised by a recent decision of a British Court of Admiralty.* Nor was the aggravated nature of the crime for the trial of which a tribunal may be instituted a cogent motive for assenting to the principle of subjecting American citizens, their rights and interests, to the decision of foreign courts; for although Great Britain, as Sir S. Canning remarked, might be willing to abandon those of her subjects who defied the laws and tarnished the honour of their country by participating in this traffic, to the dispensation of justice by foreign hands, the United States were bound to remember, that the power which enabled a court to try the guilty, authorized it also to pronounce upon the fate of the innocent; and that the very question of guilt or innocence was that which the protecting care of their constitution had reserved, for the citizens of the

* Alluding, doubtless, to the judgment of Lord Stowell in the case of Le Louis.

Union, to the exclusive decision of their own countrymen. This principle had not been departed from by the statute which had branded the slave-trader with the name and doomed to the punishment of a pirate. The distinction between piracy by the law of nations and piracy by statute was well known and understood in Great Britain; and whilst international piracy subjected the transgressor guilty of it to the jurisdiction of any and every country into which he might be brought, or wherein he might be taken, statute piracy formed a part of the municipal code of the country where it was enacted, but could only be tried by its own courts.

There remained the suggestion, that the slave-trader captured under the mutual concession of the power to make the capture might be delivered over to the jurisdiction of his own country. This arrangement would not be liable to the constitutional objection which must ever apply to the jurisdiction of the mixed commissions or of the Admiralty Courts of the captors; and if Sir S. Canning's letter was to be understood as presenting it in the character of an alternative to which his government was disposed to accede, Mr. Adams was authorized to say that the President considered it as sufficient to remove the obstacle which had precluded the assent of the United States to the former proposals of the British Government, resulting from the character and composition of the tribunals to which the question of guilt or innocence was to be committed.

The objections to the right of search, as incidental to the right of detention and capture, were also in a very considerable degree removed by the introduction of the principle that neither of them should be exercised, except under the responsibility of the captor in costs and damages to the tribunals *of the captured party.* This guard against the abuse of a power so liable to abuse would be indispensable ; but if the provisions necessary for securing effectually its practical operation, should reduce the right itself to a power merely nominal, the stipulation of it in a treaty would serve rather to mark the sacrifice of a great and precious principle, than to attain the end for which it would be given up.

In the objections heretofore disclosed to the proposed concession of the mutual right of search, the principal stress was laid upon the repugnance which such a concession would meet in the public feeling of the country, and of those to whom its interests were intrusted in that department of its government, the sanction of which was required for the ratification of treaties. The irritating tendency of the practice of search and the inequalities of its probable operation were only slightly noticed by Mr. Adams, and had been contested in argument, or met by propositions of possible palliatives, or remedies for anticipated abuses, in Sir S. Canning's letter. But the source and foundation of all these objections had been scarcely mentioned in their former correspondence. They consisted in the very nature of the right of search at

sea, which, as recognised or tolerated by the usage
of nations, was a right exclusively of *war*, never
exercised but by an outrage upon the rights of
peace. It was an act analogous to that of searching
the dwelling-houses of individuals on land. The
vessel of the navigator was his dwelling-house;
and, like that, in the sentiment of every people that
cherished the blessings of personal liberty and
security, ought to be a sanctuary inviolable to the
hand of power, unless upon the most unequivocal
public necessity, and under the most rigorous personal responsibility of the intruder. Search at sea,
as recognised by all maritime nations, was confined
to the single object of finding and taking contraband
of war. By the law of nature, when two nations
conflict together in war, a third, remaining neutral,
retained all its rights of peace and friendly intercourse with both. Each belligerent, indeed, acquired by war the right of preventing a third party
from administering to his enemy the direct and immediate materials of war; and, as incidental to this
right, that of searching the merchant-vessels of the
neutral on the high seas to find them. Even thus
limited, it was an act of power which nothing but
necessity could justify, inasmuch as it could not be
exercised but by carrying the evils of war into the
abode of peace, and by visiting the innocent with
some of the penalties of guilt. Among modern,
maritime nations an *usage* had crept in, not founded
upon the law of nature, never universally admitted,
often successfully resisted, and against which all

had occasionally borne testimony by renouncing it in treaties,—of extending this practice of search and seizure to *all* the property of the enemy in the vessel of a friend. The practice was, in its origin, evidently an abusive and wrongful extension of the search for contraband; effected by the belligerent, because he was armed; submitted to by the neutral, because he was defenceless; and acquiesced in by his sovereign, for the sake of preserving a remnant of peace rather than become himself a party to the war. Having thus occasionally been practised by all as belligerents, and submitted to by all as neutrals, it had acquired the force of an usage, which, at the occurrence of every war, the belligerent may enforce or relinquish, and which the neutral may suffer or resist, at their respective options.

Mr. Adams forbore to enlarge upon the farther extension of this practice, by referring to injuries which the United States experienced when neutral, in a case of vital importance; because, in digesting a plan for the attainment of an object which both nations had equally at heart, it was desirable to avoid every topic which might excite painful sensations on either side. He had adverted to the interest in question from necessity,—it being one which could not be lost sight of in the then present discussion.

Mr. Adams farther observed, that such being the view taken of the right of search, as recognised by the law of nations, and exercised by belligerent powers, it was due to candour to state that his government had an insuperable objection *to its extension by treaty*, in any manner whatever, lest it might lead to consequences still more injurious to the United States, and especially in the circumstances alluded to. That the proposed extension would operate, in time of peace, and derive its sanction from compact, presented no inducements to its adoption. On the contrary, they formed strong objections to it: every extension of the right of search, on the principles of that right, was disproved. If the freedom of the sea was abridged by compact for any new purpose, the example might lead to other changes. And if the operation of the right of search were extended to a time of peace as well as war, a new system would be commenced for the dominion of the sea, which might eventually, especially by the abuses to which it might lead, confound all distinctions of time and of circumstances, of peace and of war, and of rights applicable to each state.

The United States had, on mature considerations, thought it most advisable to consider the slave-trade as piracy. They had thought that it might, with great propriety, be placed in that class of offences; and that by placing it there, they would more effectually accomplish the great object of suppressing the traffic than by any other measure which they could adopt.

To this measure none of the objections which had been urged against the extension of the right of search appeared to be applicable. Piracy being an offence against the human race, had its well-known incidents of capture and punishment by death by the tribunal of every country. By making the slave-trade piratical, it is the nature of the crime which draws after it the necessary consequence of capture and punishment. The United States had done this by an act of Congress, in relation to themselves. They had also evinced their willingness, and expressed their desire, that the change should become general by the consent of every other power, by which it would be made the law of nations. Till then, they were bound by the injunction of their constitution to execute it, so far as respects the punishment of their own citizens, by their own tribunals. They considered themselves, however, at liberty, until that consent was obtained, to co-operate, to a certain extent, with other powers, in order to ensure a more complete effect to their respective acts; they placing themselves severally on the same ground by legislative provisions.

It was in this spirit, and for this purpose, that Mr. Adams had made to the British envoy the proposition then under consideration.

By making the slave-trade piratical, and attaching to it the punishment as well as the odium incident to that crime, it was believed that much had been done by the United States towards suppressing it in their vessels and by their citizens. If the British Government would unite in this policy, it was not doubted that the happiest consequences would result from it. The example of Great Britain, furnished in so decisive a manner, would not fail to attract the attention, and command the respect, of all her European neighbours. It was the opinion of the United States, that no measure short of that proposed would accomplish the object so much desired; and it was the earnest wish of the American Government that the Government of his Britannic Majesty might co-operate in carrying it into effect.

In a despatch dated on the same day with the letter we have just analyzed, and addressed to Mr. Rush, the American minister in London, Mr. Adams recapitulates the incidents of the negotiation on this subject between the two governments, in 1820–21, in which the American Government had peremptorily refused to concede the right of search in the form in which it was then proposed. He stated that the sentiments of the committee of the House of Representatives, to whom had been referred the subject of the slave-trade, were different from those of the executive government in respect to the right of search; but that upon the passage of the resolution above recited, it was well ascertained that the sentiments of the House itself on that point coincided with those of the executive department, as developed in its previous correspondence with the British envoy; since the House had explicitly rejected an amendment which was moved to the resolution, and which would have expressed an opinion of that body favourable to the mutual concession of the right.

The despatch to Mr. Rush then proceeds to observe that the general subject was resumed a short time before the decease of the Marquess of Londonderry by the British minister at Washington, Sir S. Canning, who suggested that since the total disappearance of the British and American flags from the trade, as well as those of the nations which had consented to confide the execution of their prohibitory laws to the superintendence of British naval officers, it continued to flourish under the flag of France; that her laws, though in words and appearance equally severe in proscribing the traffic, were so remiss in the essential point of execution, that their effect was rather to encourage than to suppress it; and the American Government was urged to join in friendly representations to the French Government by instructing the American envoy at Paris to concur with those which the British Ambassador had been charged with making, in order to ensure a more vigilant fulfilment of the prohibitory laws. This invitation was declined from an impression that such a concurrence might give umbrage to the French Government, and tend rather to irritation than to the accomplishment of the object for which it was desired. Mr. Gallatin was, nevertheless, instructed separately to bring the subject to the notice of the French Government, and did so by an official note, communicating copies of the recent laws of the American Congress for the suppression of the trade, and especially of the act which subjected every citizen of the United States who should be polluted with it to the penalties of piracy.

Mr. Adams then refers to Sir. S. Canning's

letter to him of the 29th of January, calling upon the American Government either to accede to the mutual right of search, emphatically pronounced in his belief to be the *only* effectual measure devised, or which was likely to be devised, " for the accomplishment of the end, or to bring forward some other scheme of concert," which the British envoy again declared his readiness to examine with respect and candour, as a substitute for that of the British Cabinet.

However discouraging this call for an alternative might be, thus coupled with so decisive a declaration of belief that no effectual alternative had been, or was likely to be, devised, an opportunity was offered, in pursuance of the resolution of the House of Representatives, for proposing a substitute, in the belief of the American Government, more effectual than the right of search could be, for the total and final suppression of this nefarious trade, and less liable either to objections of principle or to abuses of practice.

This proposition was accordingly made in Mr. Adams' letter of the 31st of March, the answer to which, on the part of Sir. S. Canning, barely noticed the proposition, to express an opinion that his government would see in it nothing but an acknowledgment of the necessity of farther and more effectual measures; and then proceeded to an elaborate review of all the objections which, in the previous correspondence, had been taken by the American Government to the British connected proposal of a mutual right of search and a trial by mixed commissions.

These objections had been of two kinds : 1st, to the mixed commissions, as inconsistent with the American constitution ; and 2d, to the right of search, as a dangerous precedent, liable to abuse and odious to the feelings and recollections of their country.

In Sir S. Canning's letter, the proposal of trial by mixed commissions was formally withdrawn, and an alternative presented as practicable, one side of which only, and that the inadmissible side, was distinctly offered, namely, that of trial by the courts of the captors.

The other side of the alternative would, indeed, obviate their constitutional objection, and might furnish the means of removing the principal *inherent* objection to the concession of the right of search—that by which the searching officer is under no responsible control for that act.

But in their previous correspondence (continued Mr. Adams,) their strong repugnance to the right of search had been adverted to, merely as matter of fact, without tracing it to its source, or referring to its causes. The object of this forbearance had been to avoid all unnecessary collision with feelings and opinions which were not the same on the part of Great Britain and upon theirs; Sir S. Canning's letter, however, professedly reviewing all the previous correspondence for the purpose of removing or avoiding the American objections, and contest-

ing the analogy between the right of search, as it
had been found obnoxious to America and as then
proposed for her adoption by formal compact, Mr.
Adams had been under the absolute necessity of
pointing out the analogies which really existed between them, and of showing that as the right of
search, independent of the right of *capture*, and irresponsible or responsible only to the tribunals of
the captor, it was, as proposed, essentially liable to
the same objections as when it had been exercised
as a belligerent right. Its *encroaching* character,
founded in its nature as an irresponsible exercise of
force, and exemplified in its extension from search
for contraband of war, to search for enemy's property, and thence to search for *men* of the searcher's
own nation, was thus necessarily brought into view,
and connected with the exhibition of the evils inherent in the practice, with that of the abuses which
had been found inseparable from it.

The United States had declared the slave-trade,
so far as pursued by their citizens, piracy; and, as
such, made it punishable with death. The resolution of the House of Representatives recommended
negotiations in order to obtain the consent of the
civilized world to consider it as piracy under the
law of nations. Those who were guilty of this
offence against international law might be taken on
the high seas, and tried by the Courts of any nation.
The principle which the American Government
would wish to introduce into the system, by which
the slave-trade should be recognised as piracy un-

der the law of nations, would be, that though seiza-
ble by the officers and authorities of every nation,
the offenders should be triable only by the tribunal
of the country of the slave-trading vessel. In com-
mitting to foreign officers the power, even in a case
of conventional piracy, of arresting, confining, and
delivering over for trial, a citizen of the United
States, they felt the necessity of guarding his rights
from all abuses, and from the application of any
laws of a country other than his own.

A draft of a convention was, therefore, enclosed
by Mr. Adams to Mr. Rush, which, if the British
Government should agree to treat upon the subject
on the basis of a legislative prohibition of the slave-
trade by both parties, the latter was authorized to
propose and conclude. This *projet* was not, however, offered to the exclusion of any other which
might be proposed on the part of the British Government, nor any of its articles to be insisted on as
a *sine quâ non*, excepting that which made the
basis of the whole arrangement to consist in the existence of laws in each country, rendering liable
their respective citizens and subjects to the penalties of piracy for the offence of slave-trading, with a
stipulation to use their influence with other states
to the end that the trade might be declared to be
piracy under the law of nations. It was only from
considering the crime in the character of piracy
that the United States could admit the visitation of
their merchant-vessels by foreign officers for any
purpose whatever; and, even in that case, only un-

der the most effective responsibility of the officer for the act of visitation itself and for every thing done under it.

Mr. Rush was instructed, in case the sentiments of the British Government were averse to the principle of declaring the slave-trade piracy by a legislative act, not to propose or communicate the *projet* of convention. He would understand its objects to be two-fold; to carry into effect the resolution of the House of Representatives, and to meet the call so earnestly urged by the British Government for a substitute for its proposal of the mutual right of search. The substitute, by declaring the offence piracy, carried with it the right of search for the pirates, as existing in the very nature of the crime. But to the concession of the right of search, distinct from that denunciation of the crime, the objections of the American Government remained in all their original force.

It was subjoined in this despatch that it had been intimated that the proposition for recognising the slave-trade as piracy under the law of nations had been discussed at the Congress of Vienna, and that the American cabinet was expecting the communication of the papers on this subject promised by Lord Liverpool to be laid before Parliament. Although the United States had been much solicited to concur in the measures of Great Britain and her allies for the suppression of the trade, they had always been communicated to the American Government as purposes consummated, to which the *accession* of the United States was desired. From the general policy of avoiding to intermeddle with European affairs, they had acquiesced in this course of proceedings; but in order to carry into effect the resolution of the House of Representatives, and to pursue future discussions with great Britain, it was obviously proper that communications should be made to the American cabinet of the progress of European negotiations for accomplishing the common purpose, whilst it was still in deliberation. If the United States were to co-operate in the result, it was just that they should be consulted, at least with regard to the means which they were invited to adopt.*

It will thus be perceived that the American executive government and legislature of 1823–24, although sincerely desirous of co-operating with Great Britain for the suppression of the slave-trade, continued to repel the proposition of a mutual concession even of the limited right of search, as a means to that end, so long as it was coupled with the consequence of carrying in the captured vessel for adjudication before a tribunal of the captor's country, or before a mixed commission composed of judges appointed jointly by both countries. To the former they objected, as identical with the exercise of the belligerent right of search in time of peace, attended with all its known abuses, of which the American people had already had sufficient experience; to the latter, as subjecting their citizens to be tried before

* Nile's " Weekly Register," vol. xxvi. pp. 347–353.

tribunals partly foreign, and thus to be deprived of those securities guaranteed by their happy constitution and laws. The American cabinet would not, therefore, consent to negotiate upon any other basis than that of the enactment of a law by the British Parliament similar to the act of Congress of 1820, by which the citizens and subjects of each country respectively should be subjected to the penalties of piracy for the offence of trading in African slaves, with a mutual stipulation to use the respective influence of the two contracting parties with the other maritime and civilized nations of the world, to the end that the African slave-trade might be generally recognised as piracy under the law of nations.

This proposal seems to be substantially the same with that made by Great Britain at the Congress of Verona, with the exception of two important distinctions in these respective plans. These are,—1st, that in the British proposal the intended concession of the right of search does not appear to have been indissolubly connected, as in the American plan, with the introduction of a new public law, by which the offence of trading in slaves should be declared piracy under the general law of nations, and thus subjected to the common jurisdiction of all maritime states, as in the case of piracy by the pre-existing law of nations. 2d, That the manner of exercising this jurisdiction was not clearly explained in the British proposal, but was probably meant to be referred to the ordinary admiralty jurisdiction of the captor's country, or to a mixed commission composed of judges jointly chosen by both parties. Whilst the American plan proposed the seizure of the offending persons and property by the commissioned vessels of war of either party for adjudication in the tribunals of that country to which the captured persons and property belonged.

The negotiation which ensued in consequence of the above instructions to Mr. Rush was finally concluded by a convention signed by him with the British plenipotentiaries, Mr. Canning and Mr. Huskinson, on the 13th of March, 1824, on the basis proposed by the American Government, of the separate laws of the two countries declaring the offence of the slave-trade to be piracy when committed by the citizens or subjects of either country respectively, with a stipulation that the contracting parties should use their iufluence respectively, with other maritime and civilized powers, to the end that the African slave-trade might be declared piracy under the law of nations. The convention provided for the mutual exercise of the right of visitation and search, under a variety of restrictions and regulations, by the commissioned naval officers of each party, duly authorized, under the instructions of their respective governments, to cruise *on the coast of Africa, America, and the West Indies,* for the suppression of the slave-trade. It farther declared that any vessel of either country carrying on the illicit traffic in slaves, might be captured by the commissioned cruisers of the other, and delivered over, together with the persons found on board, for trial in some competent tribunal, of whichever of the two countries they should be found on examination to belong to, except when the vessel in question should be in the presence of a ship of war of its own nation.

The convention thus concluded was submitted, on the 30th of April, 1824, to the Senate of the United States for their advice and consent to its ratification, as required by the American constitution in all cases of treaties negotiated by the President with foreign powers. It encountered much opposition in that body, and finally passed on the 22d of May by the constitutional majority of two-thirds of all the senators present, with the following important amendments :—

1st. The provision, extending the cruising ground of the armed vessels commissioned against the slave-trade to the coast of *America* was stricken out, so that the limits within which the right of search might be exercised were restricted to the coasts of *Africa and the West Indies.*

2dly. A provision for the trial as pirates of individuals, citizens or subjects of either party found on board a vessel sailing under the flag of a third power, was also stricken out.

3dly. A new article was proposed, by which it should be free to either of the contracting parties, at any time, *to renounce the Convention, giving six months' notice beforehand.**

The British cabinet refused to accept the altera-

* Nile's " Weekly Register," vol. xxvi. p. 233.

tions proposed by the American Senate to the Convention, and objected especially to that amendment by which the words "of America" were proposed to be stricken out of the 2d article. In the official letter of Mr. Secretary Canning to Mr. Rush, dated the 27th of August, 1824, explanatory of this refusal, it was stated that the right of visiting vessels suspected of slave-trading, when extended alike to the West Indies and the coast of America, implied an equality of vigilance, and did not necessarily imply the existence of grounds of suspicion on either side. The removal of this right, as to the coast of America, and its continuance as to the West Indies, could not but appear to imply the existence, on one side, and not on the other, of a just ground, either for suspicion of misconduct, or apprehension of an abuse of authority.

To such an inequality, leading to such an inference, His Majesty's Government could never advise His Majesty to consent. It would have been rejected if proposed in the course of negotiation. It could still less be admitted as a new demand after the conclusion of the treaty.*

In Mr. Secretary Adam's despatch to Mr. Rush, dated the 29th May, 1824, explanatory of the amendments proposed by the Senate to the Convention, it is stated that the exception of the *coast of America* from the seas, upon which the mutual power of capturing vessels under the flag of either party might

* Nile's " Weekly Register," vol. xxvii. pp. 247, 248.

be exercised, had reference, in the view of the Senate to *the coast of the United States.* On no part of that coast, unless within the Gulf of Mexico,* was there any probability that slave-trading vessels would ever be found? The necessity for the exercise of the authority to capture was, therefore, no greater than it would be *upon the coast of Europe.*† And we may add to this remark of Mr. Adams, that Great Britain is the last maritime power in the world that would consent to the exercise of the right of search, in peace or in war, upon those seas which wash her shores,—those seas over which she has ever asserted the supreme, absolute, and exclusive dominion. Well might the American Senate insist upon the exemption of the Atlantic coast of the United States from the exercise of a right of search hitherto unknown to the law of nations, when they had already suffered so much from the abusive exercise of the belligerent right of search within their very bays and harbours, especially as it was notorious that the slave-traders had ceased to frequent that coast ever since the importation had been effectively prohibited in 1808.

During the whole course of these negotiations

* And Mr. Adams might have added that the greater part of the Gulf of Mexico would be included within the denomination of the *West Indies.* Vessels of war cruising between the islands of Cuba and the southern Cape of Florida on one side, and the peninsula of Yucatan on the other, would completely intercept slave-trade in the gulf.

† Nile's "Weekly Register," vol. xxvii. p. 246.

between the United States and Great Britain, from 1818 to 1824, there is not the slightest trace of a pretention so much as intimated, much less avowed, on the part of the latter, of a right of visitation and search to be exercised on the high seas, in time of peace, for any purpose whatever, independent of special compact and the free concession of the power on whose vessels the right is to be exerted.

We now come to the treaties concluded in 1831 and 1833, between France and Great Britain, for the repression of the slave-trade, by which the right of search was first conceded by the former power for this purpose.

These conventions limit the exercise of the right thus conceded, first, to the western coast of Africa, from the Cape Verd to the distance of ten degrees south of the equator,—that is to say, from the fifteenth degree of north latitude to the tenth degree of south latitude, and to the thirteenth degree of west longitude from the meridian of Paris.

Secondly,—all around the island of Madagascar, within a *zone* of twenty leagues in breadth. Thirdly,—at the same distance from the coasts of the island of Cuba. Fourthly,—at the same distance from the island of Porto Rico. Fifthly,— at the same distance from the coast of Brazil; with the provision that the suspected vessels, descried and chased by the cruisers within the zone of twenty leagues, may be visited by them without these limits, if having kept the suspected vessels always in sight, they have not been able to reach them within that distance from the coast. The vessel thus captured to be carried in for adjudication before the competent court of the country to which they belong, there to be tried according to laws in force in that country.*

It is understood that soon after the conclusion of the supplementary Convention of 1833, between Great Britain and France, for the more effectual suppression of the slave-trade, a fresh overture was made by the British Government to that of the United States, to accede to the principle of the two treaties of 1831 and 1833, by yielding the right of search on similar terms and conditions as therein stipulated between France and England. We are not aware that the papers relating to this overture, which is said to have been made by Lord Palmerston to the American Cabinet, during the administration of General Jackson, have been published, and we are therefore unable to say whether it ever assumed the form of a serious negotiation between the two governments.

We come now to a very remarkable incident in the transactions relating to the suppression of the slave-trade. We refer to the measure brought forward in the British Parliament, in 1839, by the late ministry, to coerce Portugal into a more active participation in the accomplishment of this object. This measure, which might well be called a bill of pains and penalties against an independent state,

* Martens, nouveau recueil, tom. ix. p. 544.

although professedly aimed only at that power, was of a very sweeping and extraordinary character, as will be explained by the following extract from the debate in the House of Lords, on the 15th August, 1839.

" Viscount MELBOURNE rose to move the second reading of the Slave-trade Suppression Bill. The present state of the question rendered it unnecessary to go at any length into the details, or state the grounds upon which he hoped for their lordships' approval of that motion. Their lordships would perceive that the provisions and principles of that bill were clearly and distinctly stated in the preamble. It was to the effect, that persons who might be employed for the suppression of the slave-trade should be indemnified against actions which might be commenced against them; that the Court of Admiralty should be empowered to adjudicate on matters arising from these instructions; and also, that Government should be empowered to grant bounties, in cases of capture made under these directions of her Majesty. Among the many nations, however, under whose flag that business was now carried on, he was sorry to say the Portuguese nation stood pre-eminent. Their lordships knew how the affair stood with regard to that nation; and that, notwithstanding the treaty into which she had entered on the subject, she took no pains to carry out its provisions. He was not inclined to use any strong language on this matter; but the last notice which had been presented to the Portuguese Government by the British envoy, Lord Howard de Walden, so fully contained all the charges which might be made against that nation in this respect, that he would only call the attention of the House to that document. The noble Viscount then read the document in question, the substance of which was, an accusation on the part of the writer against Portugal, for having, notwithstanding several treaties at various periods, still continued the slave-trade, and refused to co-operate with her Britannic Majesty in its suppression. He (Lord Melbourne) conceived it unnecessary to go at greater length into that particular part of the case, and more particularly as, in an address of their lordships to the Crown, they had come to the resolution of expressing their regret, that Portugal had not co-operated with Great Britain in suppressing the slave-trade. Her Majesty had complied with the prayer of that address, and had accordingly given instructions to her cruisers to take such measures as might be necessary for the purpose alluded to, and he (Lord Melbourne) now presented that bill for a second reading, which would enable the recommendation of their lordships to be carried out.

" The DUKE OF WELLINGTON opposed the bill on the same grounds on which he had been hostile to the late measure introduced on the subject. Some of the clauses, he said, it would be impossible to carry out without a breach of all our engagements on this subject with foreign powers. He proceeded to remark, that *there were some nations, and one great nation, in particular, the United States, with whom this country had no treaties for putting down the slave-trade.* Now, as to searching the vessels of the United States for papers, if he might judge from the correspondence of the Consul at Havanna, there was every probability, not only that there would be no inclination on the part of the United States to permit the detention of their vessels, and the examination of their papers, but that that power would decidedly resist any such attempt on our part. (Hear, hear.) This was another reason, in his opinion, why measures on this subject should originate with Government, who knew what means there were for carrying the purposes of the measures into execution, rather than with Parliament. But there was another point of view on which to consider the question. The officers and persons commanding the vessels on this service, under the authority of the Lord High Commissioners of the Admiralty, were to be indemnified from all the consequences, but the state could not be indemnified. (Hear, hear.) Now their lordships might rely upon it, that for every vessel of the United States detained by our cruisers, for however short a time, this country would be held responsible for all the demurrage, and so on. The Noble Duke, after calling on their lordships not to take upon themselves the responsibility of this measure, moved that it be read a second time that day six months.

"LORD BROUGHAM must say, that the motion with which the Noble and Illustrious Duke concluded his otherwise able and most temperate speech, gave him great concern. He deemed this bill to be of the greatest possible advantage, even if larger alterations might be thought fit to be made than he had reason to believe would be necessary, and he hoped their lordships would not reject the bill in its present stage, but allow it to go to a second reading, and have alterations which might be necessarily made in committee. It could not, at the same time, be disguised, that we were peculiarly situated as to the United States, because we had not concluded any treaty with them conferring the right of search. It should be borne in mind, that the United States, at the very earliest period they were enabled to do so by the federal constitution, had adopted the abolition of the slave-trade, and were the very first to make it piracy for any one of their citizens to carry it on.

"LORD WYNFORD felt with the noble Duke, that if this bill were to pass, six months would not elapse without seeing this country at war with every state in Europe which had ships, for it could not be carried into operation except by violating existing treaties. He could not consent to the second reading of the bill, nor did he see the advantage of allowing it to go into committee, as he could not see any alteration which could be made in it, which could at all meet the objections made by the Noble Duke. (Hear.)

" The BISHOP OF LONDON said, it was with the most sincere concern he felt himself called upon to vote against the amendment proposed by the noble Duke. He had, ever since he was able to think upon this subject, been of opinion, that this *nation was especially appointed by Divine Providence, to undertake the task of putting an end to the slave-trade, and that her position amongst the maritime nations of the earth, which had given her the power, had at the same time imposed the duty of abolishing this unsanctified traffic.*

" The LORD CHANCELLOR felt perfectly satisfied that their lordships would all concur in forwarding this measure, but for a mistake into which they appeared to have been led. Noble lords seemed to think, that, by the enactments of this bill, French ships were to be searched, contrary to existing treaties. If that were the case their lordships would undoubtedly be warranted in opposing it, but these were not the enactments. The object of the bill was to direct where such search was to be made, and to exempt officers acting under the direction of her Majesty from being subject to civil prosecutions in this country for acting under those orders. Certain orders had been issued by her Majesty with respect to vessels engaged in the slave-trade ; and was it to be supposed that the officers employed in the suppression of this trade should carry out these orders at their own risk ? These orders were issued in consequence of an address presented from their lordships to her Majesty ; these orders were in accordance with that address, and their lordships were only called upon by this bill to fulfil the engagement entered into by their address, and the answer to it, and to indemnify the officers who acted under them.

" Lord Ellenborough said, that if orders had been issued, those orders should be communicated to their lordships before they were called upon to afford indemnity to those who were to act upon them.

" Lord Melbourne said, that such a course of communicating the orders of her Majesty to the House, was unprecedented.

" Lord Ellenborough thought, that in order to know what measures would be necessary, it was requisite that their lordships should be made aware of the nature of the orders which had been issued.

Lord Minto said, that of all the astounding doctrines he had ever heard, was that which called upon her Majesty's ministers to explain the terms of the instructions which had been sent out to her Majesty's cruisers (hear, hear, from the ministerial benches ;) such a demand as this had never before been made, and he could not see how their lordships should now require to be put in possession of instructions which were given, as the noble Duke himself had admitted they should be given, on the sole responsibility of the Government. There was nothing, he contended, in the present bill, calculated in the slightest degree to excite the jealousy of the government of the United States, which was as anxious as we were to put an end to the slave-trade ; nor did the bill warrant the commission of any act which was not as fully warranted without it. The real question was, whether or not their lordships would co-operate in carrying into effect the address to which they had already ageeed ?

" Lord Denman, and Lord Colville, supported the bill, which was approved by Lord Wicklow.

" Their lordships then divided, when the members were—

Contents . . . . . 39

Non-contents . . . 28

Majority for bill . . 11

" The bill was accordingly read a second time."*

It is well known that this bill was subsequently dropped by the Government in consequence of the insuperable difficulties it encountered in its passage. This attempt to enforce the abolition of the slave-trade, against other independent states, by a British Act of Parliament, must appear the more extraordinary, as the complete exemption of the merchant vessels of one nation from every species and purpose of search by the armed and commissioned cruisers of another on the high seas, in time of peace, independent of special compact, had never been drawn in question in the various negotiations on the subject of the slave-trade between Great Britain and other maritime powers, the United States included, from the peace of Paris, 1814, to the signature of the treaty of 1833, with France.   Every line of each document, and every word of each conference, implies, in the strongest manner, that no such notion had ever entered the minds of any one of the distinguished sovereigns, statesmen, and civilians, who had bestowed their attention on this important matter.

Not only so, but it is directly at war with an

London " Times," August 16th, 1839.

official communication made by Lord Palmerston
to the government of the Republic of Hayti, under
date of the 27th of January, 1840, a few months
after the Portuguese slave-trade suppression bill
was brought into the House of Commons by his
lordship. In this communication, which is quoted
by Mr. Stevenson, in his note to Lord Palmerston,
of the 27th of February, 1841, the latter refers to a
law passed in 1839, by the Haytian Government,
providing that any vessel, whether Haytian or otherwise, found in the act of slave-trading, should be
seized and brought into a port of the Republic for
adjudication. The communication states, that—

" Her Majesty's Government wishes to draw the attention of
the Haytian Government to a matter of form in this law, which
may possibly give rise to embarrassments. The law enacts, that
all vessels, whether Haytian or foreign, which may be found in
the act of slave-trading, shall be seized and brought into a Haytian port. Now, Hayti has undoubtedly a full right to make such
an enactment about her own citizens and ships, but her Majesty's
Government apprehend that Hayti has no right to legislate for the
ships and the subjects or citizens of other states. That in time of
peace, no ships belonging to one state have a right to search and
detain ships sailing under the flag of, and belonging to another state,
without the permission of such state, which permission is generally
signified by treaty ; and if Haytian cruisers were to stop, search,
and detain merchant vessels sailing under the flag of, and belonging to another country, even though such vessels were engaged in the slave-trade, the state to which such vessels belonged
would have just grounds for demanding satisfaction and repara-

tion from Hayti, unless such state had previously given to Hayti, by treaty, the right of search and detention."

The first time we hear of such a pretension, as that repelled by the British Government in the above communication, being brought forward by that Government in a diplomatic form, is in the correspondence between Mr. Stevenson, the American Minister in London, and the late and present British Secretaries of State for Foreign Affairs, the Lords Palmerston and Aberdeen.

As the documents containing this correspondence are before the public in an accessible form, having appeared in almost all the public journals of both Europe and America, we deem it superfluous to subject the papers to that full and minute analysis which we have thought necessary in respect to the previous communications between the two Governments on the same subject. We shall therefore endeavour to collect, in a summary form, from the entire correspondence, the real nature and import of the British pretension. In doing this, we think it but fair towards the British Government to bestow more particular attention on the note transmitted from the Foreign Office to the American Minister in London, since the late change of ministry; not because we do not, privately speaking, attach an equal importance to documents written and signed by Lord Palmerston, as to papers proceeding from under the hand of his noble successor in office. All that we mean to say, is, that as our country has to deal in this momentous matter with the *present* British Government, it is more important for us to determine what are its real views and intentions in respect to the question, so far as they can be collected from its official language, than to make the subject of commentary and criticism expressions which we fain would hope were hastily and incautiously used, in conference or in correspondence, by the eminent statesmen who lately filled the office of Secretary of State for Foreign Affairs.

The several cases of American vessels seized by British cruisers in the African seas present examples, but too flagrant, of the abuses to which the exercise of such a right as that claimed by Great Britain on this occasion may be liable. The proceedings of the British cruisers on the coast of Africa, in one of these cases in particular (that of the *Mary*,) is justly described by Mr. Stevenson, in his correspondence with Lord Palmerston, "as wanting nothing to give them the character of a most flagrant and daring outrage, and very little, if any thing, to sink them into an act of open and direct piracy." Indeed, this attempt to exercise the rights of war in time of peace must not only be attended with all the evils consequent upon the exercise of the right of search for enemy's property and contraband of war; but as Lord Stowell has so justly observed, has an inevitable tendency to lead to "gigantic mischief and universal war," by provoking forcible resistance on the part of the navigator, whose commerce is thus interrupted by the uncontrolled violence of foreign cruisers. The abuse of a right, such as the belligerent right of visitation and search, which all nations have occasionally exercised in turn, and none have at any time denied (at least so far as respects contraband and blockade) to be authorized by the *customary*, if not by the *natural* law of nations, may not be attended with the same fatal consequences as are to be apprehended from the exercise of the right now claimed. The exercise of the belligerent right of search may be effectually controlled by the Courts of Admiralty of the belligerent state, proceeding according to their established rules in decreeing costs and damages against the captor, in cases of seizure, without such reasonable grounds of suspicion as amount to probable cause. A forcible resistance to the exercise of this right by the belligerent cruiser, on the part of the neutral navigator, may be regarded as an unlawful act of violence, and punished in extreme cases even by the confiscation of his property. But where is the maritime code which instructs us in the nature of the securities provided against the abuse of the pretended right now, for the first time, asserted in the face of the world? In what court, and by what law, is the suspected vessel to be tried? If the seizure were made in time of war, the adjudication must necessarily take place, according to the well-known law and usage of nations, in the prize-court of the country of the captor, who is responsible to his own government, whose commission he bears for his acts under that commission;

and that government again is responsible over to the neutral state, whose subjects may complain of the injury by them sustained. If the seizure be made of a foreign vessel in time of peace or of war, under the municipal laws of the captor's country, prohibiting the slave-trade, then it can only take place within the territorial jurisdiction of that state; and a seizure upon the high seas, or within the territorial jurisdiction of a third power, would be so plainly illegal, that we may lay it out of the question. The same thing may be affirmed of an attempt to seize for a breach of the municipal laws of the country to which the captured vessel belongs. If, again, the seizure be made of a British vessel, suspected to have usurped the flag and pass of a foreign state, then the validity of the seizure, and the question of jurisdiction itself must be made to depend upon the event of the trial. If, on the other hand, the seizure be made under the existing treaties between Great Britian, the Netherlands, Spain, &c., the trial must be had in the mixed-commission-court, created by those treaties—a stipulation, to the like of which the American Government has constantly refused its assent. If it be made under the treaties of 1831 and 1833, between Great Britain and France, or under the more recent treaty between the five great European powers, signed at London, on the 20th December last, the vessel seized must be delivered over for trial to the competent tribunal of the nation to which she is suspected to belong. But how can such tribunal acquire jurisdiction to determine the national character of the vessels of a third power, an absolute stranger to the compact under which the jurisdiction is to be exercised.

All this is said upon the supposition that the visitation is followed by search, and the search by seizure, and the seizure by carrying in for adjudication. If the visitation is not accompanied by search, it is an idle ceremony, and a wanton interruption of the navigator in the prosecution of his voyage. It is by search only, by examining the ship's papers, construction, and cargo, by interrogating her officers and crew, that the boarding officer can ascertain whether, in his judgment, she is employed in the slave-trade. And it is only by seizing and carrying in for adjudication, that it can be lawfully determined by some competent authority whether his suspicions are well or ill-founded. We assert, therefore, that it affords a violent presumption against the existence of such a right, that its exercise may draw after it consequences far more fatal than those attending the ordinary belligerent right of search, which may always be, and sometimes actually is, restrained by known rules of practice, which make a part of the general law of nations as founded on usage.

On examining the letter of Lord Aberdeen to Mr. Stevenson of the 13th October, 1841, we confess ourselves unable to collect from it the real nature of the distinction alleged to exist between the right claimed by the British Government and the

ordinary right of visitation and search. If his lordship has failed in expressing with sufficient clear-
ness and precision the conceptions of his own mind,
it is most certainly not for want of the requisite
talents as a writer,—since his letter is written with
the greatest terseness and elegance,—but ought
rather to be attributed to the embarrassment occasioned by the intrinsic difficulties of a bad cause
left him as an official legacy by his predecessor,
and which the joint abilities of both might well
prove insufficient to maintain. Be this as it may,
Lord Aberdeen expressly asserts that he "renounces
all pretension on the part of the British Government to visit and search American vessels in time
of peace. Nor is it *as American* that such vessels
are ever visited.

An attempt appears here to be made to distinguish between a right to *visit* and a right to *search.*
Now we have no hesitation in affirming that this
distinction has no foundation whatever in the maritime law of nations, and the usage of the Admiralty
courts of any country. The "right of visitation
and search" is the appropriate technical term
always used by British civilians to express the belligerent right—a term which has a known sense and
value, and is the exact equivalent of the term *droit
de visite* used by the continental jurists. We repeat, that if the visitation is not accompanied by
search, it is an empty mockery, and a wanton interruption of the navigator's voyage. And in con-
firmation of this assertion, we may observe that in

all the cases brought to the consideration of the British Government, by Mr. Stevenson, in pursuance of the instructions of the American Government, the visitation was accompanied with the most rigorous search of persons and papers, of vessel and cargo, followed, in some instances, by a protracted detention, and in others by a carrying into port for adjudication. We have here, then, a *practical* commentary upon the text of these official documents, which demonstrates that the right claimed is that of visitation *and* search. We may also observe, that the same remark, made by Mr. Adams, as to the concession of the right by compact, would apply to a submission to its exercise without compact; that is to say, that if the visitation be not carried out by search, it " would reduce the right itself to a power merely nominal," the submission to which " would serve rather to mark the sacrifice of a great and precious principle, than to attain the end for which it would be given up."*

But Lord Aberdeen goes on to observe in the above-quoted passage of his note to Mr. Stevenson : " Nor is it, *as American*, that such vessels are ever visited."

In answer to this suggestion, we would remark, that neither is the neutral vessel visited, in time of war, *as neutral;* but she is even visited, and captured, and detained, and carried in for adjudication, as being suspected to be an enemy, either literally

* Mr. Secretary Adams' Letter to Sir S. Canning, June 24, 1823.

such, or as having forfeited her neutral character by violating her neutral duties. Hence the formula of a sentence of condemnation in the Prize Court always declares the ship or goods condemned to be *enemy's property;* and that, in all cases, whether the property really belongs to the enemy, or is assimilated to that of an enemy by the offence of carrying contraband, by breach of blockade, or other unneutral conduct, which is visited by the Prize Court with the penalty of confiscation. It is therefore very little satisfaction to the master or proprietor of an American vessel to be told that he is not *visited as an American*, if the visitation be actually followed by the most rigorous search, by protracted detention, and by sending into port for trial; by all which his voyage may be broken up, his cargo may perish, and his crew fall victims to a pestilential climate. We are not now arguing from the abuse against the lawful use of an incontestable and well-defined right; although it appears from the documents before us that these supposed consequences are by no means imaginary. We shall, of course, be understood as only meaning to insist upon the consideration that it is perfectly indifferent to the American merchant and navigator, whether his voyage is interrupted because he is an American, and suspected of violating the laws of his own country, or because he is suspected of not being a *bona fide* American, and of violating the laws and treaties of other countries under a false garb. Supposing him to be engaged in an innocent commerce, all this is per-

fectly indifferent to him ; and even supposing him
to be engaged in a trade prohibited by the laws of
his own country, he has, as we maintain, a perfect
right to be exempt upon the high seas in time of
peace, from visitation and search, and seizure and
detention for trial, by foreign officers and foreign
courts of justice. In order to establish the contrary
doctrine, it will be necessary to show in support of
it some treaty to which his own country is a contracting party, or some public law universally recognised as forming a part of the general international
code. But no such treaty, and no such law, has, or
can be shown to exist.

Lord Aberdeen subjoins to this assurance, that
American vessels are not visited, in time of peace,
*as American*, the startling assertion that "it has been
the invariable practice of the British navy," and, as
his lordship believes, " of all the navies in the world,
to ascertain *by visit* the real nationality of merchant-
vessels on the high seas, if there be good reason to
apprehend their illegal character."

We might ask in vain for the evidence of the
existence, in point of *fact*, of this universal and invariable practice ; but the necessity for this inquiry
will be superseded, by showing that it has no sanction in *law*. And for this purpose, a reference to
the so-often quoted judgment of Lord Stowell, in
the case of the *Louis*, will be amply sufficient. In
that judgment, that learned civilian unequivocally
asserts, "that no authority can be found, which
gives any right of *visitation or interruption* over

the vessels and navigation of other States, on the high seas, except what the right of war gives to belligerents against neutrals." The assertion of Lord Stowell, that no such authority can be found, must be considered as conclusive against its existence.

But let us examine a little more closely the assertion of Lord Aberdeen. He does not state what is to be the consequence of the visitation, supposing that the suspicions excited, by whatever cause, are confirmed in the opinion of the boarding-officer, by the examination which may ensue. Visitation is but means to an end, and unless accompanied by some examination of the papers, the crew, the vessel, and the cargo, it would be (as before remarked) a mere idle ceremony, and wanton interruption of the navigator in the prosecution of his voyage, attended with greater probable injury to him, than possible advantage to the interests of maritime police. Nor is it stated what is the precise nature of the " illegal character," the suspicion of which is here assumed, as justifying the "invariable practice of all the navies in the world, to ascertain by visit the real nationality of merchant-vessels met with on the high seas." Is it, we would ask, of such an illegal character as may be manifested by acts prohibited by the laws and treaties of the country to which the vessel belongs, or by the laws and treaties of the country to which the armed cruiser belongs, or finally by the general law of nations? To each of these suppositions very distinct considerations belong ; but we will confine our observations to the last—that is to say, to the supposition that the vessel has been guilty of some offence against the law of nations, such as *piracy*, for example, by which, of course, we mean international piracy, and not merely that which is declared to be such by the municipal statutes of a particular country.

On this part of the subject we have fortunately the aid of the highest judicial authority, to confirm the conclusions of our own minds as to the legal principles which ought to be applied to it, in the judgment of the Supreme Court of the United States, in the case of the *Marianna Flora*, a Portuguese armed merchant-vessel, bound on a voyage from Brazil to Lisbon, and captured in 1821, by a gallant officer of the American navy, then employed in cruising with a public ship-of-war of the United States, under the President's instructions, for slave-traders and pirates. The capture was made, after an accidental combat between the two vessels, under mutual misapprehension, each supposing the other to be a pirate. The Portuguese vessel and cargo, being sent into an American port for trial, under an act of Congress passed in 1819, as having been guilty of a piratical aggression against the American cruiser, were restored to the claimants by the consent of the captors. The question as to costs and damages, was brought before the Supreme Federal Court in 1826, which enlightened tribunal determined, that had the Portuguese vessel been really guilty of a piratical aggression, wantonly committed on the American cruiser, the act of Congress would not only have warranted her capture, but confiscation; and that *whatever responsibility might be incurred by the nation to foreign powers in executing such laws,* there could be no doubt that courts of justice were bound to administer and obey them. The Court also repeated its former decision in the case of the *Antelope,* that the right of visitation and search of vessels, armed or unarmed, navigating the ocean, in time of peace, does not belong to the public ships of any nation. This right was strictly a belligerent right, allowed by the general consent of nations in time of war, and limited to those occasions. It was true that it had been held in the Courts of the United States, that American ships offending against their laws, and foreign ships, in like manner, offending within their jurisdiction, might afterwards be pursued and seized upon the ocean, and rightfully brought into their ports for adjudication. This, however, had never been supposed to draw after it any right of visitation and search. The party, in such cases, seized at his peril. If he established the forfeiture he was justified; if he failed, he must make full compensation in damages.

Upon the ocean, then, in time of peace, all possessed an entire equality. It was the common highway of all, appropriated to the use of all; and no one could vindicate to himself a superior or exclusive prerogative there. Every ship sailed there with the unquestionable right of pursuing her own lawful business without interruption ; but, whatever might be that business, she was bound to pursue it in such a manner as not to violate the rights of others. The general maxim in such cases was, *sic utere tuo, ut non alienum lædas.*

It had been argued that no ship has a right to approach another at sea, and that every ship had a right to draw round her a line of jurisdiction, within which no other is at liberty to intrude. In short, that she might appropriate so much of the ocean as she might deem necessary for her protection, and prevent any nearer approach.

This doctrine appeared to the Court to be novel, and was not supported by any authority. It went to establish upon the ocean a territorial jurisdiction, like that which is claimed by all nations within cannon-shot of their shores, in virtue of their general sovereignty. But the latter right was founded upon the principle of sovereign and permanent appropriation, and had never been successfully asserted beyond it. Every vessel undoubtedly had a right to the use of so much of the ocean as she occupied and as was essential to her own movements. Beyond this, no exclusive right had ever been recognised, and the Court saw no reason for admitting its existence. Merchant ships are in the constant habit of approaching each other on the ocean, either to relieve their own distress, to procure information, or to ascertain the character of strangers ; and, hitherto, there has never been supposed in such conduct any breach of the customary observances, or of the strictest principles of the law of nations. In respect to ships of war, sailing, as in the present case, under the authority of their Government, to arrest pirates, and other public offenders, there was no reason why they might not approach any vessels descried at sea, for the purpose of ascertaining their real character. Such a right seemed indispensable for the fair and discreet exercise of their authority; and the use of it could not be justly deemed indicative of any design to insult or injure those they approached, or to impede them in their lawful commerce. On the other hand, as it was as clear that no ship is, under such circumstances, bound to lie by, or wait the approach of any other ship. She is at full liberty to pursue her voyage in her own way, and to use all necessary precautions to avoid any suspected sinister enterprize or hostile attack. She had a right to consult her own safety, but at the same time she must take care not to violate the rights of others. She might use any precautions, dictated by prudence or the fears of her officers, either as to delay, or the progress, or course of her voyage; but she was not at liberty to inflict injuries upon other innocent parties, simply because of conjectural dangers. These principles seemed to the court the natural result of the common duties and rights of nations navigating the ocean in time of peace. Such a state of things carried with it very different obligations and responsibilities from those which belonged to public war, and was not to be confounded with it.

It had also been argued that there was a general obligation upon armed ships, in exercising the right of visitation and search, to keep at a distance out of cannon-shot, and to demean themselves in such a manner as not to endanger neutrals. The court stated that it might be a decisive answer to this argument, that here no right of visitation and search was attempted to be exercised. Lieutenant Stockton did not claim to be a belligerent entitled to search neutrals on the ocean. He did not approach or subdue the *Marianna Flora* in order to compel her to submit to his search, but with other motives. He took possession of her, not because she resisted the right of search, but because she attacked him in a hostile manner, without any reasonable cause or provocation.

The Court, applying these principles to the case in judgment, determined that the gallant officer before it, was not, under the circumstances, liable in costs and damages for seizing and bringing in the Portuguese vessel, which, by her own improper conduct had led him into the mistake he had committed.* But, after all, the captor was in this case (to use an expression of Lord Stowell) "saved as by fire;" and the extreme caution the Court manifest, in limiting the right of public armed vessels cruising for pirates and slave-traders on the high seas, to the mere authority of approaching suspicious vessels for the purpose of ascertaining their real character,

* Wheaton's Reports, vol. xi. pp. 39, 40. The *Marianna Flora.*

by any means short of actual visitation and search,—
shows what would have been its opinion of the pretension now advanced by the British Government,
of a right to ascertain, by visitation and search, the
national character of such vessels.

Lord Aberdeen proceeds in his letter of the 13th
October, 1841, to Mr. Stevenson, to state the particular nature and extent of the British claim of a
right of *visitation*, as he insists upon calling it, on
board vessels navigating the high seas in time of
peace.

> " In certain latitudes, and for a particular object, the vessels,
> referred to are visited, *not as American*, but either as British ves-
> sels engaged in an unlawful traffic, and carrying the flag of the
> United States for a criminal purpose, or as belonging to states
> which have by treaty ceded to Great Britain the right of search,
> and which right it is attempted to defeat by fraudulently bearing
> the protecting flag of the Union; or, finally they are visited as
> piratical outlaws, possessing no claim to any flag or nationality
> whatever."

We may be excused for neglecting the qualifi-
cation of the right thus claimed, by limiting it to
certain latitudes and to a particular object, because,
if the right exist, it may be extended at the pleasure of the power claiming it to both the great
oceans which encircle the globe, and to any other
object which it may hereafter suit the ever-craving
appetite of dominion to embrace within its grasp.
We will, therefore, only observe that here are three

classes of cases enumerated, in which the right of
visitation and search (for such we have shown it to
be) may be exercised under the British claim. The
first class is that of *British* vessels engaged in an
unlawful traffic, and seeking to screen their offence
under the American flag. The second consists of
*vessels belonging to other states*, which have by treaty
conceded to Great Britain the right of visitation
and search, and which right is attempted to be defeated by fraudulently bearing the protecting flag
of the United States. The third comprises *piratical
outlaws*, possessing no rightful claim to any flag or
national character whatsoever.

The British Secretary of State for Foreign Affairs
asserts that none of these classes of vessels have
any title to be exempted from the exercise of the
right of visitation and search claimed by Great
Britain. He adds, that if the visitation by a
British cruiser " should lead to the proof of the
American origin of the vessel, and that she was
avowedly engaged in the slave-trade, exhibiting to
view the manacles, fetters, and other usual imple-
ments of torture, or had even a number of these
unfortunate beings on board, no British officer
could interfere any farther." That is to say, if the
vessel in question turns out, in the judgment of the
British boarding officer, to be *bonâ fide American*,
she must be released, although the proof be ever so
clear that she was actually engaged in the slave-trade.

But, we would respectfully ask, what if she
proves, in the judgment of the boarding officer, re-

sulting from an examination of her papers and other proofs, to fall within one of the above-described classes of vessels—that is to say, to be a British vessel disguised under the mask of the American flag and papers; or to belong to some one of the States which have, by treaty, conceded to Great Britain the right of visitation and search; or, finally, to be what Lord Aberdeen calls a *piratical outlaw?* What farther proceedings are to be had in either or all of these cases? There can, we conceive, be but one answer to this question—namely, that the vessel, thus visited and searched, must be carried into some port of some country, for trial before some court of justice. As before observed, the visitation would be a worse than idle ceremony, unless followed by search, and the search a wanton outrage unless the vessel were to be carried in for adjudication, in case she turned out, in the judgment of the boarding officer, not to be American, and at the same time to fall within some one of the categories above enumerated. Now, this is precisely what happens in the exercise of the belligerent right of visitation and search, in time of war. If a vessel sailing under the neutral flag is boarded and examined by a belligerent armed and commissioned cruiser, and the result of the examination establishes her neutrality in the judgment of the boarding officer, or his superior commander, she is of course released, and suffered to pursue her voyage. But if, on the other hand, their *prima facie* judgment be, that the ship or cargo is in reality enemy's property, or that the

latter is contraband of war, or that the proprietor
or master have been guilty of some unneutral act,
by which the property is rendered liable to confiscation, the vessel is, of course, detained, and sent in
for trial in the competent Prize Court of the captor's country. The identity of the right, now for
the first time claimed by Great Britain, with the
belligerent right of visitation and search, which
Lord Stowell asserts, and Lord Aberdeen admits,
cannot exist in time of peace, thus becomes more
and more evident at every step we advance in the
progress of our investigation.

We repeat, if the seizure had been made in time
of war, the captured vessel must be carried into
port for adjudication before the competent Prize
Court of the captor's country. But it being made
in time of peace, the captured vessel, if belonging to
the first of the classes above mentioned, and seized
and proceeded against as a British vessel engaged
in violating the municipal laws of Great Britain,
must necessarily be tried before the Court of her
own supposed country. But what if she proves, on
trial, to be an American, though guilty of slave-
trading?—and what, if she turns out to be both
American, and innocent of all offence ? If there
should have been, in the opinion of the Court by
which the vessel is tried, such reasonable grounds
of suspicion as constitute probable cause of seizure,
the owners would not, according to the usual course
of the Admiralty, even be entitled to costs and
damages for the detention, which, in most cases,

must be attended with the loss of the voyage. The discretion of that Court is exercised in giving or refusing costs and damages, in cases of marine torts, with such arbitrary latitude, and is formed by such merely equitable, and even politic considerations, that it would be a very unsafe reliance for a foreign claimant to look to for adequate indemnity in case of wrongful seizure. In short, it would be easy to show the multiplied embarrassments that must inevitably arise from this anomalous attempt to execute the laws of a particular state beyond its own territorial jurisdiction on the high seas, in time of peace, upon vessels suspected to be its own, and to have fradulently assumed the flag and papers of another nation. In time of war, such vessels may be seized and proceeded against in the exercise of a right incident to that of belligerent capture. Being once brought before the Prize Court, such vessels might be condemned on the ground that a British subject has no *persona standi in judicio* to claim property taken in the act of violating the municipal laws of his own country, whilst the claim of the American citizen would be at once rejected as founded in fraud and supported by falsehood. It is plain that the condemnation in the Court of Admiralty cannot proceed upon such grounds in time of peace. Doubtless, the laws of trade and navigation of any particular country may be executed by the seizure of the vessels proved to belong to that country, in a place which is not within the territory of a particular state, such as the high seas. But such seizure must necessarily be made at the hazard of mistaking the property of the citizens of another nation for that of the subjects of the state under whose authority the seizure is made. The right, then, claimed by Great Britain, so far as respects the first class of cases enumerated by Lord Aberdeen, comes to this:—that it is a right to seize at the peril of the captors, subject to full compensation in costs and damages, in case the property turns out to be American as claimed, and there be not such reasonable grounds of suspicion as constitutes what is technically called *probable cause* of seizure. There being no treaty and no public law applicable to the case, against whom can the costs and damages be decreed by which the injured party is to be indemnified? Who is to pay them, the captor or his Government? Under the special contracts entered into between Great Britain and other powers, the jurisdiction to try is conferred upon the tribunal of that nation to whom the vessel appears, *prima facie*, by the flag under which she sails, and *by the flag alone*, to belong; and the costs and damages which may be allowed by such tribunals, in case of wrongful seizure, are to be paid by the Government of the captor.* The neglect of the British Government to provide an adequate indemnification for the losses and injuries already sustained in the various cases of seizure of American vessels in the African seas,

* Convention of the 22nd March, 1833, between France and Great Britain, Articles 1—7. (Martens' " Nouveau Receuil," tom. ix. pp. 550—553.)

affords but little encouragement for the United States to acquiesce in the pretension of another nation to determine for them, without their special consent, the national character and proprietary interest of vessels navigating the high seas in time of peace under their flag and papers.

If, on the other hand, the seizure be of a vessel appertaining to the second class, that of vessels supposed to belong to States which have, by treaty, conceded to Great Britain the right of visitation and search, the trial must be had before the court of the country to which the vessel is supposed to belong, or before a Mixed Commission, as the one or the other tribunal may have been provided by the compact. But how can either of these tribunals acquire jurisdiction over the vessels of a nation which is no party to the treaty ? In one of the cases mentioned in Mr. Stevenson's correspondence, that of the *Jago*, sailing under the American flag and papers, the vessel was sent into the British port of Sierra Leone for trial before the British and Spanish mixed commission at that place, which very properly refused to take jurisdiction of the case. But suppose a vessel, suspected to have fraudulently assumed the American flag and papers, to be sent in for adjudication before the Court of the country to which she is believed in fact to belong, under the Treaties of 1831 and 1833, between Great Britain and France, or under the quintuple treaty of the 20th December last; and suppose she proves, on trial, to be *bona fide* American, against whom are the costs and damages to be decreed, supposing the seizure not to be justified on the ground of probable cause? Not against the British captor, for the Court has no jurisdiction over him, except in the case of seizure of a vessel belonging to the nations who are parties to the treaties—not against his Government, for the United States are no parties to the treaties; and one of their citizens can claim no rights under the treaties.

It thus appears that, in the cases supposed of an attempt to execute the treaties against the vessels of a nation, which is no party to the compact, that such nation is placed in a much worse situation than if it had actually acceded to its stipulations. Instead of remaining under the tutelary protection of the pre-existing law of nations, which exempts its vessels on the high seas from the jurisdiction of every other nation, and from all search and detention in time of peace, it is involuntarily exposed to the exercise of the right of search, in the same manner, and to the same extent, with those States who have conceded the right by treaty; and *that,* without those securities against the but too probable abuse of the rights which are provided by the compact to which it is no party. The British claim, then, is, in effect, a claim to do that independent of the compact, towards those who are no parties to the compact, which the compact, for the first time, authorized to be done towards any independent nation whatsoever. To justify such pretension, no arguments drawn from mere considerations of convenience, expediency, or even necessity, can avail to supply the intrinsic legal defects of the pretension itself. Even if it were ever so clearly proved, that the African slave-trade could be effectually suppressed by the concession of the right of search on the part of all nations; which is so far from being proved, that the direct contrary is conclusively demonstrated by fact and experience, according to the opinion of one of the most distinguished enemies of the traffic, it would not follow that even so great a good can lawfully be accomplished, by acting towards any one nation, even the smallest and the weakest, as if it had freely made the concession. Considerations of higher convenience, expediency, and necessity, connected with settled views, of policy as to national honour, and rights and interests, stand in the way, in the opinion of at least one great maritime nation, of its accomplishment by the means proposed. The words of Lord Stowell before quoted, here apply with all their force of energetic expression and intrinsic wisdom: "No nation has a right to force its way to the liberation of Africa, by trampling on the independence of other States; or to procure an eminent good by means that are unlawful; or to press forward to a great principle, by breaking through other great principles that stand in the way."

We do not say that the matter in controversy is not a proper subject of international legislation to be undertaken at some auspicious moment; but we do say, so far as the United States are concerned,

that the negotiation, which must precede the introduction of a new public law of Europe and America
for the regulation of this matter, cannot be undertaken on the basis of the previous admission of the
claim now set up by Great Britain, under the pre-
existing law of nations. Such an admission would
have been peremptorily and unanimously rejected
by the Powers, who, after long hesitation and repeated refusals, have at last concurred in making
the mutual concession of the right of search, under
certain qualifications, the ground-work of a more
comprehensive compact on this important question.
This compact is not yet consummated, between the
European Powers who are parties to it, by that
final sanction, which is necessary to make it obli-
gatory, even among them. The signature of the
quintuple treaty of the 20th December last, appears to have been anticipated by the President of
the United States, in his message to Congress, of
the 7th of that month.* The President, at the
same time, anticipated the answer, which the Cabinet of Washington cannot fail to give to all the
arguments which may be advanced from the Bri-

* " Whether this Government should now enter into treaties
containing mutual stipulations upon this subject, is a question for
its mature deliberation. Certain it is, that if the right to detain
American ships on the high seas can be justified on the plea of a
necessity for such detention, arising out of the existence of treaties between other nations ; the same plea may be extended and
enlarged by new stipulations of new treaties, to which the United
States may not be parties."

tish Foreign office, as to the supposed necessity of exerting the right claimed by Great Britain, under the pre-existing law of nations, in order to give more complete effect to the treaties already entered into, or which may be entered into between her and other European States, to which treaties the United States, are and may long remain utter strangers.

As to the third class of vessels supposed by Lord Aberdeen to be justly liable to visitation and search on the high seas in time of peace, that of "piratical outlaws possessing no claim to any flag or nationality whatever," we would merely observe that, if by the term *piratical outlaws* be meant those who are guilty of piracy under the law of nations, the judgment of that enlightened tribunal, the Supreme Court of the United States, in the case of the *Marianna Flora*, above quoted is amply sufficient to dispose of that class of cases, and to show that the piratical character of vessels navigating the ocean must be ascertained by means other than the exercise of the ordinary right of visitation and search. In fact, the character of pirates, properly so called, is seldom difficult to be determined. These enemies of the human race do not wait to be visited, but either fly from pursuit, or commence a piratical aggression against those who would approach for the purpose of ascertaining their real character. The present maritime police is amply sufficient to protect the peaceful navigator against sea-rovers; and there is, in truth, no more reason for admitting the exercise of a general right of visitation and search, in

order to discover, arrest, and punish pirates, than
there is to require all travellers to be examined and
searched; because there are occasionally some highway robberies committed in every civilized country.
The offence of piracy is in fact, at present, extremely
rare on every sea: and the United States have found
no difficulty in effectually putting it down in the
American seas, without asserting an indiscriminate
right of search; they do not claim it for themselves,
for any purpose, and they will not acknowledge it
in others.

But if by "piratical outlaws" be meant persons
engaged in the slave-trade, which, though formerly
tolerated, and even encouraged by every nation, is
now forbidden by the municipal laws of all civilized
and Christian countries, and is declared to be piracy, and as such visited with capital punishment
by the laws of some States; we would remark, that
it does not therefore follow that the offence of trading
in slaves is deemed piracy under the law of nations,
and as such punishable in the Courts of any country into which the offenders may be brought. The
attempt to introduce a new public law, making the
offence piracy, under the law of nations, failed at the
Congress of Verona; it failed in the negotiations of
1823-4, between the American and British governments, although the former was extremely anxious
to make it the basis of a general concert among the
the States of Europe and America; it failed in the
more recent negotiations between the five great
European Powers, which finally resulted in the

treaty of the 20th December last. It is, therefore, a looseness of language, fatal to all accurate reasoning, to call slave-traders "piratical outlaws," and to assert that, for the sake of discovering and punishing these persons as offenders against the law of nations, a general right of search is to be assumed in time of peace, as if cruising against slave-traders were to be put on the same footing with public war between sovereign communities.

It is quite clear that such a right can never be established but by the voluntary consent of all civilized States. The equality of nations in the eye of that public law by which the great community of Christendom is held together, forbids the idea of any, even the smallest and weakest State, being coerced to consent to the establishment of a new rule of international conduct. The supposition that the five Great Powers of Europe intended, in their recently-projected compact, conceding the mutual right of search, to bring to bear upon America the moral weight of this Holy Alliance against the traffic in human beings, in order to compel her to sacrifice her maritime rights to this object, is, therefore, wholly gratuitous and inadmissible; and if there be any of the intended contracting parties who had such a design in view in procuring the assent of others to the proposed compact, they are probably, by this time, convinced that the attempt will be vain. The United States adopted the European law of nations when they separated from the British empire. But it was the internal law of Europe, as it stood on the footing of immemorial usage and approved practice, and recognised by public jurists of authority, at the time when the United States declared their independence of Great Britain. To borrow the language of the President's message already referred to:—

"However desirous the United States may be for the suppression of the slave-trade, they cannot consent to interpolations in the maritime code at the mere will and pleasure of other governments. We deny the right of any such interpolation to any one, or all the nations of the earth, without our consent. We claim to have a voice in all amendments or alterations of that code; and when we are given to understand, as in this instance, by a foreign government, that its treaties with other nations cannot be executed without the establishment and enforcement of new principles of maritime police, to be employed without our consent, we must employ a language neither of equivocal import, nor susceptible of misconstruction. American citizens prosecuting a lawful commerce in the African seas, under the flag of their country, are not responsible for the abuse or unlawful use of that flag by others; nor can they rightfully, on account of any such alleged abuses, be interrupted or detained on the ocean; and if thus molested or detained, whilst pursuing honest voyages, in the usual way, and violating no law themselves, they are unquestionably entitled to indemnity."

Though the United States do not consider themselves bound by innovations, made, or attempted to be made, without their consent, in the maritime law of nations, since they became an independent power, they do not the less desire to see substantial improve-

ments effected in that code by the general assent of
all civilized states. Pacific and commercial from
inclination and habit, the American people wish to
see the same rules applied to hostilities by sea which
have so long contributed to mitigate the ferocity of
war by land. For this purpose they have ever
sought, in their treaties of navigation and commerce with other nations, to abolish the usage of
seizing and confiscating enemy's property in the
ships of a friend—that relic of a barbarous age,
when maritime warfare was identified with piracy,
by the ferocious manner in which it was carried on;
and by which usage the peaceful intercourse of
commercial nations with those who continue to be
their friends, though involved in war with others, is
still interrupted, in the midst of the general efforts
of a more enlightened period to adopt a milder system of international relations. Influenced by these
considerations, the United States, in the first commercial treaty they formed with any foreign power,
that with France, of the 6th February, 1778, recognised the principle of free navigation in time
of war, by adopting the maxim—*free ships, free
goods;* which had been incorporated into the conventional law of Europe, ever since the Peace of
Utrecht, 1713, though seldom or never observed in
practice towards neutrals by any of its maritime
states, when actually engaged in hostilities with
each other. France, soon after, became involved
in the war between Great Britain and her revolted
colonies; and the French government issued, on

the 26th July, 1778, an ordinance extending the stipulations of the treaty of the 6th February to all neutral states. The cause of American independence, and of the free navigation of the seas, thus became blended together, and was supported by the joint efforts of France, Holland, and Spain, sustaining the late British colonies in their struggle for emancipation. The armed neutrality of 1780 was formed by the neutral powers of the Baltic for the purpose of more accurately defining the rights of free navigation, and its principles were acknowledged by all the maritime states of Europe. The American congress recognised these principles by its ordinance of 1781, for the direction of the American cruisers and courts of prize. The war of the American Revolution was at last terminated by the treaty of peace signed at Versailles in 1783, by which the independence of the United States was acknowledged by Great Britain, and the treaties of Utrecht, by which the freedom of neutral navigation was stipulated, were renewed and confirmed between Great Britain, France, and Spain. In 1785, the United States concluded a treaty of commerce and navigation with Prussia, in which not only the same liberal principles of the maritime law of nations were recognised, but other stipulations intended to mitigate the evils of war by land and by sea, were inserted by the American negotiator, Franklin, who carried into diplomacy the enlightened spirit of the philosopher and philanthropist. On the breaking out of the war of the French Re-

volution in 1792–3, in which nearly all the powers
of Europe became involved, the United States sought
in vain to preserve those privileges of neutral commerce and navigation which had been guaranteed
by solemn treaties with the maritime states of the
European continent. Great Britain would not acknowledge them in theory or in practice; and those
very powers which stipulated to respect them, *re-
membered to forget* their own professions and pro-
mises, in their anxiety to crush a dangerous and
formidable enemy, who "attempted to propagate
first her principles, and afterwards her dominion,
by the sword."* Hence the mutual interdictions of
neutral trade with each other, in corn and provisions, published by the different belligerent powers;
hence the revival by Great Britain of the rule of the
war of 1756, interdicting all neutral commerce with
the colonies of an enemy; hence that foul brood of
paper-blockades, and orders in council, and imperial
decrees, by which European warfare was brought
back again to the barbarous practices of the darkest
age, and by which series of innovations and interpolations into the public code of nations, all neutral
commerce was ultimately prohibited, and America,
the only remaining neutral nation, was herself reluctantly compelled to take part in the war. During
all this period, the right of visitation and search con-

---

* Mr. Canning's despatch to Sir C. Stuart, 28th January,
1823. (British Annual Register, Vol. LXV. *Public Documents*,
p. 141.)

tinued to be asserted by Great Britain, not only for
its original purpose of seizing enemy's property on
board neutral vessels, and for executing these barbarous edicts, but, in the case of the United States,
by impressing from under their flag those seamen
whom the British officers, in the exercise of an
arbitrary discretion, chose to denominate British
subjects. Had the practice of impressment, thus
exercised as an incident to the belligerent right of
visitation and search, been in fact applied to *British*
seamen only, the American Government might
have longer forborne to resist the application of a
principle against which it had never ceased to pro-
test. But when to the other violations of its maritime rights, was superadded the application of the
right of search to the impressment of *American*
citizens, thousands of whom were detained and
compelled to fight the battles of Great Britain
against nations with whom their own country was
at peace, the American Government could no
longer hesitate to draw the sword in order to vindicate the honour of its national flag. Hence its
invincible repugnance to recognise by express compacts, to any extent or for any purpose, a right,
which, whether applied to MERCHANDISE or MEN,
is so capable of being abused by a gigantic naval
power. It is one thing to admit the right of visitation and search, as applied in time of war for its
original, legitimate objects, recognised by usage and
by the positive, if not by the natural law of nations;
and it is another and very different thing, to consent

to extend that right to a state of peace, and to objects foreign to those for which it was originally established. The United States have never pretended that Great Britain could lawfully be compelled by force to abandon the belligerent right of visitation and search, however anxious they may have been to establish by general compact the maxim, of *free ships, free goods*, by which the exercise of the right would be limited to the sole cases of contraband and blockade only. On the other hand, it cannot be pretended that the United States may be compelled by force or by that moral duress which is equivalent to the application of force, to abandon the immunity of their flag from the exercise of that right in time of peace. Their conclusive objection to its extension by special compact, in peace or in war, in any form, and under any restrictions, which have heretofore been proposed, is not merely that it may be liable to abuse, as experience has but too well proved ; but that such express recognition might involve by implication the establishment of maxims relating to neutral navigation, the reverse of those which they have ever sought to incorporate into the international code by the general concurrence of maritime states. "The encroaching character of the right, founded in its original nature as an irresponsible exercise of force," with its tendency to grow and gather strength by exercise, render it the more necessary, in their opinion, to be cautious in furnishing fresh precedents of its extension to new objects, and to a larger sphere of operation. It was, therefore, with great satisfaction, that we recently heard the assurance solemnly given from the legislative tribune, by the constitutional organ of the French Government, in respect to foreign relations, that " the United States were free, and would remain free," in regard to this matter. That is to say, as we understood the declaration, that the liberty of action of the American Government remains entire; that it will neither be constrained to accede to the treaties concluded, or to be concluded between the European powers for the mutual concession of the right of visitation and search, nor compelled by any of the contracting parties to submit to the exercise of that right as a measure deemed indispensable to the effectual accomplishment of the object of those treaties.*

* " Messieurs, les Etats-Unis sont libres, ils resteront libres." (M. Guizot's Speech in the Chamber of Deputies, January 24th, 1842.)